GO FISHING FOR
SKATE
& RAYS

GRAEME PULLEN

The Oxford Illustrated Press

The Oxford Illustrated Press
© 1991, Graeme Pullen

ISBN 1 85509 222 0

Published by:
The Oxford Illustrated Press, Haynes Publishing Group, Sparkford,
Nr Yeovil, Somerset BA22 7JJ, England

A catalogue record for this book is available from the British
Library.

Printed in England by:
J. H. Haynes & Co Limited, Sparkford, Nr Yeovil, Somerset

Contents

Erratum
The second caption on the fifth
page of the colour section refers to
the illustration facing page 73.

Dedication

To Alan Dingle, top Cornish skipper.

Acknowledgements

I would like to thank the following for their help in the preparation of this book:

Mr Norman Dunlop, Central Fisheries Board, Republic of Ireland.

Mr Duncan Swinbanks, Knotless Fishing Tackle Ltd.

Angling Foundation and Glasgow Museum (for information on common skate).

International Game Fish Association, Fort Lauderdale, Florida, USA.

British Record (Rod-Caught) Fish Committee.

Introduction

The quality of tackle and technology for sea fishing has improved significantly over the last fifteen years. Gone are the days of solid glass, stubby rods, a mixture of brass booms for terminal gear and an old wooden centrepin. The British sea angler has come of age, and with this new tackle he can extract the utmost pleasure, not just from our harder-fighting game fish but from what were previously a fairly mediocre species.

Better charter boats with full fish-location equipment and longer distance capability have put more distant grounds within reach of the average angler, and if the cost of a place aboard today's charter boat has risen, at least it is value for money. Most anglers are prepared to pay more for their fishing if they know their chances of a successful trip are high. The modern charter boat can pinpoint potential fish-holding grounds close to shore or 30 miles out to sea. This is due to the popularity of wreck fishing in the early seventies, when accuracy of anchoring was of paramount importance—too far from the wreck and you caught nothing, too close and you lost your terminal gear. As the commercial fishermen made use of the latest electronic wizardry from the orient, the charter skippers followed suit.

Thirty years ago there were perhaps more fish about, but location remained the key to success. Without the aid of fish-location equipment many charter skippers remained within sight of land so that they could use landmarks as bearings for finding a good spot again. Once out of the sight of distinguishable landmarks, the chances of finding the same good fishing spot twice was worse than slim. Now, once a good area has been pinpointed, the charter skipper can punch in the co-ordinates, and record the exact location for future use. Offshore banks, sandbars and rough ground areas can now be fished properly, thus opening up new areas to the fishermen.

Even shore fishing has seen an increase in catches for those prepared to spend the time and money to invest in the latest rod and reel. The

Go Fishing for Skate & Rays

What an incredible haul! A total of SEVENTEEN thornbacks landed from the shore by the author (right) and two other anglers. The fish were kept alive in rockpools for this photograph, then returned to the water. The mark was at Clifden in Ireland.

advancement of carbon as a rod-building material is well documented elsewhere, but now with modern reels, a good style of casting and modified terminal tackle, the beach and rock angler can, like the boat fisherman, reach new grounds and marks by distance casting. More magazines pin-point good fishing areas. Better bait storage and presentation enable the shore man to travel out armed with the best he can get. Even though many species are coming under increasing pressure from commercial overfishing and pollution, I believe the time has never been better to put a few fish on the beach.

Sea fishing is a year-round sport, dictated only by the weather. As some species fall into decline, the modern sea angler should look to 'lesser' species to give him some sport. The big flatfish families have long been popular with anglers, but now the conservation-minded among us may not wish to throw every species in the fish box. Admittedly the fact that a returned fish that has every chance of then being scooped up in a netter's trawl seems strange, but tagging programmes have shown that fish can survive capture to be caught again.

Introduction

Skate and rays fall into the category of big flatfish, and they represent some of the most popular species around the British Isles. The true leviathans, the common skate, are for the most part rare, but can be taken fairly consistently in Scotland and Ireland. They rarely migrate long distances, and tagging research has shown that stocks can be decimated if a whole catch is killed. Charter boats specialising in fishing this giant now have scales on board, so that after a quick weighing and photograph, that huge fish can be slipped back over the side, and perhaps caught again the following year, none the worse for wear.

Big halibut are possibly the hardest-fighting of the big flatties, and they are quite a rarity. I would imagine that few are ever returned alive if they are caught on rod and line, as the flesh is very highly prized in the market. When an unseen fish departs at high speed after breaking up an angler's tackle, it could well be a halibut. In future years I can see the pursuit of this species becoming very popular, with special expeditions mounted for them.

While big common skate and halibut grab the headlines with their size, the thornback skate and the various species of rays make up the 'bread and butter' of the sea angler. Personally I derive greater pleasure from catching a thornback from the shore than from a boat, and provided conservation measures are adhered to, the rays will be around long enough to put a decent bend in the rod. Providing you use light to medium tackle for catching them, they offer good sport, but while you might want one or two to take home for the pot, put most of them back. Pressures on all stocks are increasing, and it surely is common sense not to kill everything you catch. Rays in particular seem to have a high survival rate if unhooked properly, so invest in the future a little: *Go Fishing for Skate and Rays* is intended to increase your knowledge and skill, and in doing so, it might help conserve the species too.

About the Fish

Identifying fish can seem like a nightmare especially when you consider that the most recent fish classification lists around 21,000 varieties. Of these the skates and rays can be the very devil to sort out as there are literally hundreds of variations that baffle anglers with their similarities and colorations. Incorporated in the order of Rajiformes are the huge manta rays—unlikely to be fairly caught on rod and line—sawfishes and guitar fishes. The latter can be caught on rod and line, and several have been landed recently in The Gambia, a destination frequented by the British package tour industry.

The differences between skate and rays often cause confusion, and what you call a species often depends on what part of the British Isles you come from. I have always called the thornback, for instance, a skate, yet in Ireland it is called a ray. It appears that they are all in fact rays, but are divided into two categories: the long-nosed rays, which are called skate, and the short-nosed rays, (including all the smaller species) which are called rays. Skate and rays are definitely a species on their own however. While they have been likened to bottom-swimming sharks, it is the dogfish that are more closely related to the shark, and the rays are more like flattened dogfish. The 'misfit' is the monkfish, which has similarities to both sharks and skate.

Skate and rays are recognisable by their flat appearance, and they are classified for their skeletal configurations, the blending of the pectoral fins to the body and their well-developed eyes, located on the top of the head. From the location of the eyes it can be seen which species spend their time lying on the sea bed, partially covered with sand, with the obvious need to have their eyes clear of the sand.

Some skate and some rays are smooth-skinned, others have prickly curved thorns, especially near the tail. Yet others are rough, and many have a poison sac in the base of their tail. The larger manta ray can reach

Wing-gaffing skate appears to do them little harm, and it is better than lifting by the trace if no net is available. This hookhold could easily pull free if too much pressure is applied.

the staggering weight of over 3000lb, with a wing breadth of well over 20ft. Sawfish, also a member of this order, reach spectacular proportions, often as long as 20ft.

The development of the young is oviparous in the skate family, and ovoviviparous in all other members of the order. The former means that fertilisation is done internally with the eggs cased in a tough capsule which is commonly seen washed up on the high tide line of beaches. Ovoviviparous means that the young actually develop inside the oviducts of the female until they are ready for extrusion, but there is no placental attachment.

Skate and rays are generally slow movers, but when they are alarmed they can propel themselves along at some considerable speed. The method of propulsion for most of them is an undulating movement of the wings, similar to that of a bird, depressing the trailing edge of the wings from front to back in a repetitive motion; the faster they flap the faster they go. The torpedo ray is the exception and waddles along the bottom.

Electric rays are primarily fish eaters, stunning their prey with an electrical discharge. The eagle ray will swim near the surface but spends its feeding hours on the sea bed. The manta has apparently adapted to swimming near the surface feeding on plankton, shrimp or tiny mullet which it directs into its cavernous mouth by two large protrusions called cephalic fins. The majority of skate prefer somewhat shallow water, but the North Atlantic abyssal skate, *Raja Bathyphila*, is one of the really deep-water species. It has been taken at depths of 7000ft.

The skate family is called *Rajidae*; the electric rays are *Torpedinidae*, the stingrays *Dasyatidae* and the eagle rays *Myliobatidae*. The Greek word for the electric ray was *narke*, from which our own word 'narcotic' was evolved.

Edibility

If you buy skate in a fish and chip shop, you are probably buying thornback skate. They are netted commercially, though in Ireland they hardly merit a second glance from either anglers or commercial fishermen. This is all to the good for the thornie population, and may be the reason why they are so prolific off this coastline.

Many of the rays must be edible, although they are not a popular food. It may be only an old wives' tale, but I've heard that the eagle ray in particular should be avoided because their habit of feeding on oyster and mussel beds is supposed to give their flesh a higher level of heavy metals and pollutants if they are caught near a polluted area. It never ceases to amaze me how many countries, our own included, still continue to dump sewage and pollutants far out to sea in the hope it will be dispersed by tidal currents and deep water. They must surely realise that they are poisoning our fish and introducing poisons into our food chain.

The nutritional value of fresh fish, if cooked properly, compares favourably with meat, and there are cultures that live almost entirely on fish. With a deep freeze, catches can be labelled with the date caught and stocked until required. Many anglers go fishing just to fill their freezer, but if you just enjoy catching the fish why not return some alive? If you do freeze fish, make sure you gut them as soon after capture as possible and keep them cool, or better still, chilled. This is easier today than it was before the advent of cool boxes with thermal insulation. Igloo is a good make of cool box, and if you go to the United States, take advantage of some of their offers on coolers, some of which have thermal inserts in the lids and bases.

A company called ASW Coolfish Bags also has a good range of thermal zip-up bags which are ideal for transporting fish. They feature a washable inner lining, and you can chill them down using a blue pack you can get at most camping shops. Pop them in the freezer overnight, then into the bag

11

Top ray skipper Vincent Sweeney shows off a Co. Mayo thornback skate. Winged and skinned, the skate makes a regular appearance on the fishmonger's slab, or in the local fish and chip shop.

when you leave for your fishing trip, and they should keep your fillets or whole fish chilled until you get home.

When you remove the wings from skate and rays you should pop each wing into a freezer bag before you put them into the cool box or ASW bag. A large wing can be divided into steaklets and being flat, they stack neatly. If you cook them from fresh, it is best to leave them in the fridge overnight to allow the ammonia in the meat to seep out, but if they have been frozen you can cook them immediately.

Using a sharp knife, cut the wings into strips to make portion-sized pieces, skin them and then soak in salt water. This is supposed to draw out any taints in the meat, which will then remain white. Perhaps the salt accelerates the dissolution of ammonia in which case it is a good idea to soak them if you intend eating them immediately.

To cook a skate wing, you must first skin it. You can skin a raw one using pliers and a towel to prevent slippage, but an easier way is to par-boil the wings for about four minutes. The skin then comes off easily with a blunt knife, but take care to avoid cutting or generally disturbing the meat. Remember that fish cooks fast, but if the portions are from a bigger small-eyed ray, partial cooking in boiling water will help, especially if you intend to fry them.

Once you have removed the skin, pat the fish with dry paper towelling to soak up any excess moisture. Beat up an egg in a bowl, dip the fillet of wing in, then roll it in dry breadcrumbs. Deep fry it in cooking oil and serve it with hot chips, making sure that your plate has been pre-heated. As well as cooking quickly, fish meat tends to cool rapidly, so serve it as soon after frying as possible. Deep frying is by far the best way to cook skate or ray. Skate and ray meat is tender and the cartilage bone is safe to give to the dog. Considering that he would never have seen a ray or skate in the wild, it never ceased to amaze me how quickly our Jack Russell could dispense with the remnants of a skate wing!

The 'eyeballs' of the skate, are considered something of a delicacy. Technically these 'eyeballs' are not the eyes used for seeing, but are the cheek muscles which the skate and ray family use to such good effect when crunching up food between their plate-like jaws. These muscles are considerably stronger for their size than one would imagine, and breadcrumbed then fast fried, they are regarded more highly than the wings.

It has been said that the female skate out of season is poor to eat, but I am not sure quite what 'out of season' means. I can't see the commercial fishermen checking each skate before it goes into fish cakes, so I assume that this is a fallacy.

The French way to cook skate is to cut them into five-ounce portions, cook them in strong salted water and vinegar, then when drained, cut the flesh off the bone. The meat is then kept hot in cooking liquor and served with melted butter. Fish cakes can also be made from skate, when added to mashed potato and a little of the liquor the fish was cooked in. Season to taste.

The liver of the skate is considered a delicacy and can be served either hot or cold. Cook as for the meat, in boiling water, but add carrot and onion, parsley, thyme and a bay leaf. It will take little more than three minutes to cook. Serve cold with a vinaigrette dressing or hot with a spoonful of the cooking liquor over it.

Halibut are prime eating fish as the price on a restaurant menu will confirm. Should you be fortunate enough to catch one, or even fancy trying it from the fishmonger's slab, the following might be of assistance. It is good boiled like skate and served with hollandaise sauce. But personally I like to deep fry it in breadcrumbs, then just when it looks good, shallow fry it at a lower heat in white wine. The outside will be crispy but will have a soft flavour from the wine.

Fried fillets of the Pacific halibut are great favourites with anglers in the

United States. The meat is firm enough to make mock scallops by cutting the meat into cubes, dipping them in beaten egg, breadcrumbing them and placing them in a deep-fat fryer. Serve with tartare sauce, a squeeze of lemon and some white wine, and friends will be lining up at the door!

A final tip is to lay some bacon in a baking tray, spread sliced onion over it, then lay a 2-lb slab of halibut on top with a bay leaf. Pour a few tablespoons of melted butter over the fish and cook it slowly. Alternatively, pour some melted butter over the fillet, dip it in breadcrumbs and put the bacon and sliced onion on top. Wrap it in cooking foil, give it thirty minutes of moderate heat, take it out and finish it off under the grill. Serve it with jacket potatoes and you have a meal fit for a king.

But first . . . find your halibut!

The Species

Butterfly Ray

I mention this species because many anglers might want to take the short trip down to Puerto Rico in the Canary Islands, where many European line-class record rays have been recorded. My first association with the butterfly ray was here, with a fish around 94lb if I recall correctly. There are several species of butterfly ray, and they may be classified in a different family, *Gymnuridae*. The width across the wings is similar to the length of the body, and the tail is very short. The back is a brown, sandy colour, occasionally with dark lines. Their tonal variations blend in with colours of the sea bed and adapt as they move around. The common Atlantic species is the smooth butterfly ray, which may have a span of four to five feet, and is reputed not to have a stinging spine in its tail. It occurs on a line south from Cape Cod to Brazil, so there is an outside chance that one may be picked up in British waters.

The spiny butterfly ray has the same distribution area as the smooth butterfly ray but is larger and can have a span of seven or eight feet. I believe this may have been the specimen I first recorded in Puerto Rico. At the time I didn't realise that there were two species. A few years later myself and some friends were catching stingrays off the cement factory on Gran Canaria. We were enjoying a social day, resting after a blitz on non-existent marlin stocks. Wives and girlfriends were on board and because of the abundance of stingrays I started passing my rod round whenever I felt another ray flop on the bait. Most of the rays averaged about 30lb. I noticed that often the ladies didn't get them off the bottom quickly enough and then had to spend ten to fifteen minutes trying to prise them off the sand! One particular bite I passed on proved to be a 70-lb butterfly ray! It was difficult to watch the old conoflex 30-lb blank fold

Over 94lb of butterfly ray for the author. The fish fell to a bait of legered bonito and sardines.

over double and stand back as one of the women fought for fifteen to twenty minutes to bring the fish in. Needless to say we were all extremely envious!

Blond Ray

This species is one of the larger, and harder-fighting rays. Similar in appearance to the small-eyed ray, it used to be mistaken for the latter. The outline of the body is heart shaped, and there are few spines along the back. The identifying characteristic of the blond is that the small spots extend right on to the edge of the wing tips. Its back is sandy to a dark tan in colour, and it likes the sand and shell-grit of sandbanks. Blond rays can be taken from the shore but generally they are fished from a boat. They feed on small fish and crabs, catching them (like other rays) by smothering them with their flat bodies. The blond ray is a hard fighter, and if you don't get it up from the bottom the minute you strike, it will suction down

The author with a nice blond ray taken on sandbanks off Jersey, in the Channel Islands. Both blond and small-eyed ray are good scrappers on medium weight tackle.

on the sea bed until only continued rod pressure can prise it up.

The blond ray is a comparatively new species for the sea angler. Twenty years ago little was written about them, but over the space of a couple of years, West Country charter boats started to catch them from the offshore sandbanks. They like the deeper water and strong tide flows, invariably falling to either sand eel or mackerel fillet baits. There is a thin spattering of dots on the top of the sandy-coloured back, and a few spines or prickles along the underside of the wing edge. They are still sought after by the confirmed ray angler, as they may grow as large as 60lb. On average they weigh around 20lb, with 30-lb fish reported to the angling press in most seasons. They are most prolific around the Channel Islands and the West Country, seldom venturing up into the North Sea. Unlike the thornback, you will generally only find two or three together. They don't seem to be a shoal fish, and most of the time a single blond will be caught in amongst some small-eyed ray. If I had to choose a bait for them it would have to be an edible peeler crab or a couple of hermit crabs, both fished on 16-lb-test uptiding tackle coupled to a long flowing trace and running leger. The blond would be rated as one of the strongest and largest rays in the British Isles.

Cuckoo Ray

This is another of the smaller rays, but fairly easy to identify owing to the pale brown or off-yellow back and oval-shaped body. The easiest mark to look for is the almost black eye spot on each wing, with curved lines across it. They probably only run to about ten pounds, and although quite prolific in trawl-net catches, they are not seen much by anglers. This could be due to their small average size (maybe two or three pounds), since most boat anglers will have hooks and baits too large for them. Small hooks on a running leger rig and a strip of sand eel, crab or mackerel about the size of your thumb would be best suited for them. Worm baits could also be successful, but worms are only used in quantity by deep-water boat anglers when they are after cod in the winter. Rays like the cuckoo could well have migrated south by then. Worms might produce a few in summer, especially when fishing a deep-water offshore sandbank. Because of the large spines on the back, even on the small specimens, take care when holding them.

Eagle Ray

This species has been recorded in British waters, and it grows to a good size. It has a very long whip-like tail, with a poisonous barbed spine just near the base of the tail. When boated or beached it lashes its tail like a bull whip, but the only danger is in the spine. Snap it with pliers before unhooking the fish.

The eagle ray is reputed to grow to a huge size, especially in warm waters, where it occurs with some regularity. The back colours range from brown/grey to a light black, depending on the habitat. Eagle rays are different from other species, as the head is located away from the flat body, and is raised up. It also swims higher in the water than the other rays, though it returns to the sea bed for the bulk of its feeding. It has also been called the bat ray. The wing tips are pointed, and flat teeth form the crushing plates. The suggested maximum weight is 400–500lb—an incredible fish for a rod and line enthusiast.

The distribution of the species is from the eastern Atlantic up to the British Isles, right down past the Mediterranean to South Africa. It has even been a guest in trawlers' nets in the North Sea. It has a tendency to feed on mussel and oyster beds, so anglers in Britain would do well to think of fishing these habitats—though they are normally to be avoided as tackle losses are high.

The Species

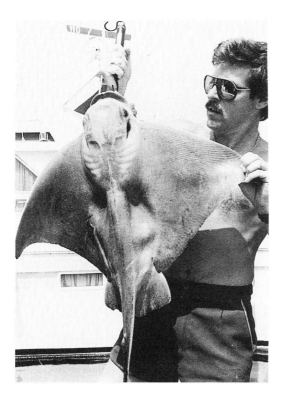

The author admires a good eagle ray taken on sardines. Note the humped forehead on this species.

They are graceful swimmers, and more than one ocean diver has been shocked to see one of them 'flying' towards him in the water. They have poisonous spines, but they are located very near the base of the tail, which makes it difficult for them to stab into anything. They can be unhooked safely, but care must be taken not to tread on the spine or stab yourself.

The spotted eagle ray may carry up to five spines and is dotted all over, making it attractive to look at. Although running to 500lb, it is seldom encountered by rod and line anglers.

The Atlantic cownose ray, which is part of the eagle ray family, is more commonly found by fishermen. Their wingspans average three feet but can be as large as six feet, and they are the more common species, living in both warm and cool waters. The species has large cow-like eyes, and remains alive for a long time out of water. Apart from keeping your first or largest fish, I see no reason to keep them—weighing and photographing aboard the boat is sufficient, although in places like the Canary Islands they believe that any ray returned alive will finish the day's sport. This of

19

course is not true. The same used to be said of freshwater bream, and I have tipped 180lb of bream back into a swim and still gone on to catch more!

Electric Ray

There are more than thirty species of electric rays in the world, but because they live at great depths they are seldom seen, even by deep-water commercial trawlers. They can grow to over six feet in length and two hundred pounds, while others are barely a foot in length. The first electric ray I saw was in the lamplight of the boat jetty in Black River Bay, Mauritius. I knew immediately that it was an electric ray, because of the short, paddle-like tail with twin dorsals. One of our group caught it a night later, and reported that he received a shock similar to the shock from a car engine's spark plug when he came to unhook it.

Extensive research has been done on the electrical charge from these rays and it has been discovered that they have special electric organs, or muscles, in the front half of the body. Each unit acts as a battery, the lower plate negative, the upper positive. All the units can discharge at once if the ray wishes, and as many as a million generating units in the two organs can, in a large ray, emit a charge of 200 volts. If shocks are repeated immediately, the charge gets weaker. They use it to stun prey. The electric ray tends to lie in the sand or mud until an unwary fish or crustacean passes over it. Then it kills the prey with a charge before eating it.

The Atlantic torpedo ray runs to about thirty pounds in weight, but can grow up to 200lb. The torpedo ray I saw that night in Mauritius was anything but fast, waddling its way from side to side over the sand as it searched for food. The back colour is a dark chocolate brown, and the body outline, apart from the tail, is almost circular. Sport from these is minimal unless you fish with light line, and even then you run the risk of the ray burying itself in the sand if you don't have the tackle power to lift it. It does have a comparatively larger mouth though, and will take big baits.

Halibut

Of all the big flatfish species, the halibut is possibly the hardest-fighting of them all. It is even rated as a game fish by the International Game Fish Association in Florida, and has record listings for both the Californian and the Atlantic varieties. The three main species of this incredible flatfish

The Species

The Atlantic halibut grows to a great size, and is the largest of the flatfish species. This specimen was landed from the Stellwagen Bank off Massachusetts, USA, by angler Thomas Lemon. (*Photo: IGFA, Florida, USA*).

are Atlantic halibut, Pacific halibut and Californian halibut. There is a species called Greenland halibut, but as far as I know it has never been recorded on rod and line.

Hippoglossus Hippoglossus is the largest flatfish in the world. It is recorded that in Grimsby in October 1957 a monster halibut weighing 540lb, and estimated to be sixty years old was docked. It is also the largest of the bony fish, and inhabits the cold waters of the North Atlantic, across to Iceland and Greenland. The largest known specimen I can find reported was taken in Sweden and weighed 720lb. An eight-foot halibut would push the scales over 350lb.

All species of halibut like cold and deep waters, but in the polar regions you only find the Greenland halibut. The skin is smooth like many smaller flatfish, and the back is a marvellous olive green to drab brown. The lateral line curves above the pectoral fin. It is a species that responds well

The Pacific halibut is smaller in average weight than its Atlantic cousin, but seem to have even more vivid markings. This $37\frac{1}{2}$-lb fish was caught by Roger Jones from California. (*Photo: IGFA, Florida, USA*).

to long-lining rather than trawling, particularly around the Faroes and Iceland. Here the hook baits are herring or small coalfish, but almost any small fish may do. Anglers hooking a small fish and then finding it grabbed by a large unseen adversary always think the adversary is a shark. However, when this happens in the waters around Scotland, and particularly if the 'take' occurs within the first few turns of the reel handle, I am sure it is the halibut that is the culprit. Halibut are immensely strong and possess a stamina that none of the other skate and rays have. This may be due to the skeletal structure of the fish and its lean, narrow shape. Certainly the massive tail acts like a paddle when it fights, and runs are powerful, almost unstoppable.

They eat other fish or crustaceans, and have a large extendable mouth with well-developed teeth on either jaw. Tagging research has revealed that this species makes extensive migrations, interchanging with stocks on the western side of the Atlantic. Spawning, water temperature and availability of prey, however, will keep them in one area for a longer time. They appear to like broken ground rather than the clean sand that the rays and skate love. This is because the halibut can swim fast and catch fish directly in its field of vision, whereas rays and skate have to flop on to baits or fish before they can locate them with their mouths. The halibut has well-developed sight, with eyes located just behind the jaws; this allows it to hunt over broken rocky ground where it can easily grab prey that the rays and skate cannot. Trawlers only catch them occasionally, as they are loath to lose expensive netting gear on rocks. This is why long-lining is successful for them.

Eggs can be laid between April and August, depending on locality, winter conditions and water temperatures. The males, like many species, are smaller than the females. Females mature at about ten years old and their maximum lifespan is believed to be forty-five years, although I find that an incredibly long time to escape both the complex nets and the long lines around our coasts. Halibut meat is highly prized, and the fish is a valuable catch for any commercial fisherman.

Scotland, Orkney and the Shetland Isles are prime areas to try for halibut, but if you want to catch one on a rod and line, take a trip to the west coast of America and fish for the Californian halibut. This species rarely tops 60lb, but it provides great sport on light tackle. Drift fishing with live anchovies is a localised method, but slow trolling with lures has also been effective, since halibut will lunge at anything that flashes in the water.

The Californian halibut's cousin, the Pacific halibut can be found from the Bering Sea to California. This species is highly migratory: through tagging research it has been found that adult specimens have swum as far as 2000 miles, but it is not known whether this is for feeding or migration purposes. The Pacific halibut shows just how much the species loves cold water. In northern areas they frequent shallow water as the temperature there is low, but the further south they go the warmer the water becomes and the deeper they go—right down to 600 fathoms if necessary. Stomach contents have revealed that they feed on midwater baitfish as well as from the sea bed, though whether this is because the baitfish sometimes swim nearer the bottom, I'm not sure.

The north-west coastline of Ireland is probably one of the untapped areas for any rod and line fishing, let alone specialised halibut forays, and it could be the venue of the future. The only report I could find of halibut in Ireland came from before the war off Valentia Island on the west coast. In 1926 a Mr Henning landed three halibut in one day, weighing 152, 128 and 120lb, quite an astonishing catch. I fished there for shark only last year, but I had no idea it had been a halibut hotspot! I was impressed by the rough ground and deep water, so the next time I spend a day there drifting a bait it will be on the bottom, not just below the surface.

Fishermen off the south coast of Ireland have also reported halibut catches, but perhaps global warming will increase water temperatures and push the species further north. This is why I think the Donegal and Sligo coast might be the place to try. Southern Ireland is well known for its fine mixed fishing, but the far north of the country still has many areas to be explored. Tory Island in particular looks to be a classic halibut area. While the smaller flatfish family like flounder, dabs and plaice feed on crabs and tiny shellfish, the halibut feeds on lobsters and big edible crabs as well as fish. Perhaps there may be a case for using a whole edible peeler crab as bait when anchored, but still adding a flasher spoon uptrace of the bait to draw the attention of any passing fish.

Iceland is also a good venue, and competitions there have yielded rod and line specimens of 100lb. The method was to drift with a dead bait of herring.

As the optimum water temperature for halibut has been reported as being about 35°F, you could attach a thermometer that records and locks in a reading to your terminal gear and drop it down to check the temperature before you begin fishing. It could save a lot of wasted time.

The halibut's main features are the curve in the lateral line above the pectoral fin and the broad tail. Normally the eyes are positioned on the right side of the head but reversed fish are not uncommon. After the eggs have hatched, the small fish look just like any other, but after a period of several days they start to tilt to one side. The eye on the lower side then starts moving up and across the rest of the head until both eyes are on top. Whereas the skate and rays have eyes that are centred on the top of the head, the halibut, like all flatfish, have both eyes slightly to one side. As the eye moves, so the skull twists as well, and the mouth rotates 90°. With the fish now turned on its side, the pigmentation in the skin of the lower side becomes lighter, and the upper side darker. Finally you have an entirely flat fish with a white underbelly and darker back.

The flesh of the halibut is in such demand that in recent years attempts have been made to farm it. As a female of 150lb can lay up to two million eggs, it can be seen that with a controlled environment, a successful farming venture could be highly profitable.

Spotted Ray

This is the smaller cousin of the ray family, and one you would be hard pressed to classify under the 'sporting' category. It represents a very small proportion of ray catches, and in many areas should be regarded as something of a rarity. I have taken only a few, mostly off the Isle of Wight, when I have been using small baits for whiting and gurnards. In appearance the spotted ray is not dissimilar to the blond ray, but it is small, only running to a few pounds. It has a covering of spots on its sandy-coloured back (fewer than on the blond) which do not run off the edge of the wing tips. There are no spines on the underside trailing edges of the wing tips.

Spotted rays are common in parts of the English Channel, round the south-west corner from Sussex and Kent up into the Thames Estuary. Their breeding habits are similar to the other rays, and they appear to prefer warmer southern waters. Indeed, they might just be a fringe Mediterranean species, with the south coast of England being the northernmost limit of their range.

It is said that the spotted ray is good eating, but so few seem to be caught, I doubt there are many anglers who have had the chance to taste them.

The longer nose of the spotted ray avoids any confusion with the blond ray. In Ireland, particularly the west coast bays, the spotted ray, known also as the Homelyn ray can be taken with some regularity; one of the best places to try is Blacksod Bay. I have fished several ray sessions with Vincent Sweeney, manager of Blacksod lighthouse, from his old boat the *Girl Emer*. His favourite Homelyn mark was just out from the pierhead by the first buoy, and while I was interested in taking the thornbacks, Vincent had his eye on setting a new record for Homelyn. We took a few, but nothing above 5lb, and my own enthusiasm was somewhat limited.

Sandy Ray

This is a ray that few anglers see, and when they do it can be mistaken for the blond. I often wonder whether there is any interbreeding between rays that so closely resemble each other, but only the scientists can tell us. The nose of the sandy ray is slightly pointed, and the overall shape is not dissimilar to the cuckoo. There are small white spots on the back—the only break in an otherwise uniform sand or tan colour. There may be distinct differences between the male and female of the species, with the male having spines on the upper edges of the wings.

An inhabitant of the English Channel, it is another species that I feel is a Mediterranean species on the fringe of its northernmost limit. Sandy rays are seen more in trawl nets than on an angler's line, and I feel that they are a reef-ranging ray working in the open spaces of clean ground frequented by the trawlers. As the angler will generally be looking for some sort of feature on the sea bottom, it could be that he will simply never place his bait in the area of this ray.

Stingray

The stingray is possibly the best of all the ray family. In recent years there has been a growth in the popularity of this species. It is definitely a tropical species, with the southern half of England and Ireland as the northernmost limit of its range. About twenty years ago it was rare even to read of a commercially caught fish, but as the temperatures of our oceans rise as one of the effects of global warming they seem to be appearing in ever increasing numbers. Stingers can be taken from both shore and boat, but they should be regarded as an isolated species. Although they probably move about the entire length of the English Channel, there are only a few places for the shore angler to try for them—around Portsmouth and Southampton and on the east coast at St Osyth beach. The premier bait to use is the king ragworm, and I cannot help wondering if the stingray move over ragworm beds specifically to feed on this bait. From the boat angler's viewpoint the stingrays can be localised, and the best marks are closely guarded secrets; pinpoint accuracy is needed in anchoring. They are a warm-water species, so June, July and August are the best months to fish for them in the British Isles.

They have a round appearance, and can range from a drab brown to almost black, although it should be noted that in the tropics many different species can be caught. The species gets its name from the whip tail which carries a venomous spine. Unsuspecting anglers may think this spine is located in the tip of the tail. It is in fact found halfway up, and consists of a straight bone with vicious barbed edges. Once driven in, I can imagine it would be very painful to extract. The stingray can whip its tail over almost to its head, so when you want to unhook it, get another angler to stand on the tip of the tail, and snap off the barb with a pair of pliers. Any stingray you return to the water will be none the worse for wear, as the spine is used as a defence mechanism and not for obtaining food. I have seen and caught stingrays abroad that have had their whole tails cut off. They took the bait so presumably the loss of the tail doesn't inhibit their movement. However I see no reason to disfigure a fine fish when the only dangerous part is a five-inch bony spine that it doesn't use.

Previously the sting from this barb was thought to have been caused by mucus entering the wound—remember that stingrays are particularly slimy. However, it has been confirmed that there is a poison sac located at the base of the spine, and this causes major inflammation of the immediate area. It is extremely painful and can cause severe shock in certain people. It has even been known to penetrate sea boots, so care should be exercised, even when snapping the spine off.

Big as the stingray is, in tropical waters they can fall prey to sharks. Two species of shark are renowned for eating stingrays. The tiger shark

The author with his biggest shore-caught stingray at 34lb. It took a small fillet of reef fish.

has a mouth like a dragline bucket and the appetite of a starved hippo, while the bull shark is renowned for its ability to swim into freshwater rivers and despatch a few of the locals. Both species have been recorded with numerous broken stingray spines in their mouths and lower jaws, so presumably the poison in the stingray's tail doesn't bother them. Many of the stingrays without tails could be a by-catch from trawlers, and the tails could have been cut off as the fishermen disentangled them from the net.

The back of the stingray is humped, and it therefore weighs a good deal more than you might expect. A stinger that looks as though it should weigh 15lb might actually pull the scales down to 30lb. In British waters I have heard of commercially caught fish weighing 100lb, and rod and line catches of 70lb are possible. In foreign waters they grow considerably larger, and the heaviest I know of was around 460lb, taken by an angler in the Florida Keys while he was after shark using a bottom bait. A good stingray from British waters would be 30lb. In recent years there have been a few stingray reported by anglers fishing the south-west of Ireland, and should sea temperatures continue to rise I think we are going to see many more caught.

The species anglers are most likely to find around the southern British Isles is *Trygon Pastinaca*. This is the common stingray, and its distribution is thought to be the Mediterranean, the Black Sea and the eastern Atlantic from northern Norway to Madeira. It has about 100 related species worldwide. The common stingray likes calm water, generally shallow (under 200ft). A row of stumpy spines runs down the centre line of its back, varying in density from specimen to specimen, and the back can be considerably humped. The belly is a dirty white and the back light brown with a hint of smudgy yellow. It matures at around 100lb, but I have heard of very big stingrays being seen by divers looking at coral reefs which terminate in sandy bottoms. They are common around Florida, and at Islamorada I saw a photo of one in excess of 450lb. The Gulf of Mexico holds a large population of this species, presumably because of the gradual change in depths from very shallow to deep.

It is fairly common to see them in the Florida Keys, where they run over the bonefish flats on a high tide, stopping to root out any small fish or crustaceans they find. They root up the sand to such an extent that the water clouds into a milky white for some large area downtide, and they can seldom be confused with a school of bonefish 'mudding' in the same area. Some books say this is a small species of stingray, yet in Florida they have a 'rough-tailed stingray', which is surely the same species. Yet the latter runs to several hundred pounds. Perhaps there are separate sub-species.

Having mentioned that the common stingray will move into shallow water, it is worth noting that they can be found off Mauritania, on the west coast of Africa. With a backdrop of the Sahara desert, this arid area has barely any habitation, but the water, in contrast to the desert, is rich in life. Here the mineral-rich waters of the Canary's current move up over the continental shelf bringing food in the shape of plankton and small fish. The water close to shore will be warm, and while access is limited, the fishing is supposed to be superb. When conditions are calm, the angler has a good chance of taking very big stingrays, certainly up to and over 50lb, from the beach. Any excursion needs to be highly organised, however, as there is unlikely to be any rescue if things go wrong! However, stingrays, butterfly rays and a large fish not unlike America's red drum, can all be taken. Perhaps in the future a British company may offer fishing packages to this unusual destination, and give shore anglers a chance of taking large shore rays.

I took my largest shore ray in the Bahamas, from Exuma Island to be exact. I had been hoping to go bonefishing but for some reason the trip didn't come off, so I fished from the jetty in Georgetown, where several yachts were moored. Apart from barracuda and an enormous houndfish, it was a quiet morning until I spied a big stinger flopping along. An hour later and I had it hooked up, and my bent rod was weaving between the moored yachts with a half-empty spool. It was some time before I was able to drag it up the beach, by which time a crowd had gathered. The stinger was despatched with a piece of 4 x 2 timber and consumed later that same evening aboard one of the American yachts. It tipped the scales at 34lb, and was landed on an 8lb Shakespeare spinning rod!

Captain Mitchell-Hedges, in his book *Battles with Giant Fish*, describes some very big stingray. There is a photograph of a 300-pounder, and he took another of 260lb. He also boated a truly enormous leopard or whip ray, measuring 7ft 6ins across the wings and 6ft 9ins from the head to the base of the tail; the total length from the head to the tip of the tail was an incredible 16ft 3ins. The weight of this ray was recorded at 410lb. The only leopard rays I have been fortunate enough to see were in the reef entrance to the Black River, Mauritius, where I saw them leaping, presumably in an effort to rid themselves of lice. When in Bermuda I watched a large leopard ray of possibly 70lb on several occasions gliding about under the bridge at Flatt's Inlet. I tried to catch it, of course, but luck eluded me.

While boat-fishing waters, both at home and abroad may account for the larger rays, it is the clear-water fishing that I find the most exciting. You need to travel to somewhere like the Florida Keys to experience this, but the chances of making contact with a stingray are very good. The rays run the deep channels between the road bridges, but slide up on a flooding tide to feed over the bonefish flats. My first experience with one was on a bonefishing trip, on the flat closest to Bud 'N' Mary's Marina on the Atlantic side.

Guides in Florida specialise in three main species: tarpon, which hunt and travel the deep water edging onto the flats, bonefish, which are right on top of the flat, and permit. These are the 'cult' species, and anything else is ignored. Their view is that the moment you cast your shrimp at a cruising bonnet-head shark, the biggest school of bonefish seen that season will come right behind it. Fishing being fishing one can see their point of view, but anglers soon tire of spending hour after fishless hour, just looking for clouds of mudding or tailing bonefish.

The day in question saw this flat devoid of any suicidal bonefish, but alive with small sharks and rays. Our guide had spent the best part of the day watching us miss our chances of bonefish and our relationship with him had almost reached breaking point, when I suddenly saw my chance. A stingray flapped its way on to the sandy patch he had pre-baited with shrimp, ready for a school of bonefish. I could see the stinger stopping, then sending up a puff of coral sand as he grubbed out those pieces of shrimp. What a waste! I sent in a sly underhand cast, and within the minute the clutch was squealing as the reel emptied. In water barely covering them, rays can move. This one ended up being returned alive, and weighed just 10½lb, but it was still my first skinny-water stingray!

Years ago the liver of the stingray was used to make oil for lamps, and the flesh was dumped. I have eaten stingray in the Bahamas and confirm that it is certainly edible, if somewhat bland, so an exotic recipe might serve to furnish the taste buds better. The spine is sometimes dried out and stripped down for use as knitting needles. The stingray is viviparous, unlike most of the other rays.

Small-Eyed Ray

This species of ray is one of the hardest fighters I have come across. They are matched in stamina by the blond ray, and from the shore the small-eyed is a good scrapper.

The small-eyed ray seems to be more of a hunter than the thornback, and its diet consists of sand eels, small fish and crabs. They definitely prefer areas where there is a run of tide, and if this sandy area is flanked by an outcrop of rocks, so much the better. They grow well into double figures, and average between 8 and 12lb. The boat fishermen would do best to look to sandbanks which have a channel or undulation cut through them. The top lip of the bank, where the water spills over, is about the best ground to try.

As far as shore fishing is concerned, I consider this species something of a rarity from an open surf beach, but you might have a better chance casting out near a fringe of rock outcrop. Better still are some of the rock platforms that allow you to cast a big bait well out into deep water with a good tide flow pushing over it. You need to be fishing over clean ground, sand, or shell-grit. Devon and Cornwall are the areas best associated with small-eyed rays, but I have taken them on the west coast of Ireland, fishing a sandbank barely 200 yards from the Doonmore Hotel on Inisbofin Island.

They feed best in a flow of tide, and my theory for this is that small immature fish are forced down near the sea bed during strong tidal flow, where water currents are at their weakest because of the friction with the sea bed. Once slack water comes, the immature fish rise up off the bottom and the rays cannot catch them, since they are unable to flop down from above and pin them to the sea bed. For that reason I find it best to start fishing an area at the start of the flood, knowing that the slack-water period is likely to give the fewest bites.

Another point worth making is that if you use a scented bait, like mackerel strip or sand eel anointed with fish oil, the scent trail is not going to be distributed over such a large area when the tide is slack. When the

A small-eyed ray with its multitude of dots as markings.

current is pushing along it creates a mini-slick of smell that is carried a long distance, but in a narrow band. Narrow as this is, a ray will follow it up to its source and locate the bait. At slack water the area of oil will be wider, but will not stretch as far.

The small-eyed ray will chase a bait in clear water. For this reason it sometimes pays to dispense with a grip lead and just let the current bounce a plain lead bomb along the bottom. This is particularly successful if you are using sand eel. When boat fishing over a sandbank many anglers use a fixed grip lead in the uptiding technique, which is correct when the tide is pushing hard. However, when the tide eases you should try bouncing a plain bomb round as the rays will still take slowly moving baits.

Small-eyed rays seem more lithe than thornbacks, and definitely put up a better fight. Perhaps it is the stronger tidal area they live in, but their skin is also smoother to the touch and they have more protective mucus slime on them. They are a good sporting fish, especially from the shore, so you may want to return them alive for another day. The body itself is disc-shaped—very similar to that of the stingray—and the colour is light fawn or sandy. Presumably they have been caught commercially to weights far exceeding that of the present British rod-caught record which is 16lb, but I can find no record of outstanding specimens. Many years ago they were caught but confused with other species, and they have only recently become popular with boat and shore anglers.

Common Skate

This is the species most likely to attract the attention of the serious big-fish angler, for while other species of ray rarely exceed 50lb, the common skate goes to well over 200lb and hence they have always been regarded as something of a big-game fish among British anglers. Even years ago, when tackle was inadequate, a struggle with a big common skate could be the highlight of an angler's career. Today the common skate has attracted more interest than ever, and conservation measures in certain areas have induced the species to return in sufficient numbers to make them a worthwhile angling proposition.

Like all skate and rays, common skate are carnivorous, but their build indicates that they are not well suited to a fast chase for prey, although they do have a reasonable turn of speed. They cruise the bottom trying to locate their food—possibly small fish or crustaceans living under the sand—by scent and vibration. The mouth, located on the underside, is well equipped to deal with the job of crunching and grinding crabs, but they are so powerful that I wonder whether they don't use them to grind shellfish as well. They have a patterned grid of teeth, and the jaws, looking rather like large lips, are ground one against the other with powerful jaw muscles. While the teeth are not designed for cutting, the pressure the jaws can exert is quite incredible, and fingers could be crushed if the unwary angler is not careful when unhooking.

That great flat body acts like a blanket. As the skate cruises over the bottom a few inches from the sand, I believe its well-developed scent organs are used to find its prey, and once over it the skate flops down, smothering the entire area with its body, and trapping any prey beneath it. The skate then shuffles about until the prey is located by its grinding teeth.

Around twenty different species of skate have been recorded off the British Isles, many of the more unusual ones by deep-water commercial trawlers, and over 150 are believed to exist worldwide. Even the common skate has variations, with names such as bottle-nose ray, white skate, bordered skate and blue-nose skate. Other names include the flapper and Burton skate. They may all prove to be minor variations rather than independent species however, and the common skate is the single species most likely to interest the angler.

In keeping with the other ray families, the big common skate has not

The Species

One from the archives. This is the reason sport for the large common skate declined, although it should be recognised that this is still a creditable catch. The Latchford Brothers from Tralee, pose with an amazing FIVE common skate over the 100lb mark. (*Photo: Norman Dunlop, Central Fisheries Board*).

only the mouth, but also the gill openings for the intake of water on the underside. The outside gill opening, through which water is expelled, is found on the top of the fish. All the rays and skate lay egg capsules, which most of us will have seen at one time or another washed up on the high tide line of beaches. They are roughly oblong in shape with a long tendril in each corner, which one assumes is used to attach itself to the sea bed until it hatches.

The common skate may possibly reach a weight in excess of 400lb, but such a fish would surely be impossible to prise from the sea bed on ordinary boat tackle. Colorations vary little in the common skate—a brownish grey on the back, with a few black spots or blotches, and a grey/white underbelly. The tail is quite long and thorned. Although they are not as common as the name might imply, they tolerate a wide range of tidal flows. The west-coast bays of Ireland are shallow, with minimal tide, yet they provide some great skate fishing, with fish in excess of 100lb being landed.

My own opinion is that they are in fact more common than anglers realise. Ireland has a small resident population of sea anglers, and depends largely on an influx of tourists through the summer months. Skate are

33

often not found because tourists are more interested in catching smaller fish as quickly as possible, rather than sitting it out with a big bait for a single bite. Plenty of patience and a large bait are essential for the common skate enthusiast. All the bays in Ireland are productive, but I believe the skate are fairly territorial, even within the confines of the bays. Once located, they are not difficult to catch, and a chat with some commercial fishermen might reveal their whereabouts. I believe there is a good supply of untapped skate fishing in Courtmacsherry Bay, having seen photographs of skate well into three figures, that were taken from there, and all returned alive.

Moving on from Ireland the tide races of the Isle of Wight at one time saw big common skate being caught. In complete contrast to the minimal tide flow of Ireland, the English Channel is fast, yet the skate still feed. Even in its heyday, however, the Isle of Wight threw up only the odd fish, and the most reliable common skate fishing today is up in the north, around Scotland. Orkney, Shetland and northern Scotland all have fine common skate fishing, brought about by the conservation efforts of anglers and skippers alike.

Some ports have gained a reputation as being productive for the common skate fisherman. Ireland's Fenit is one. Twenty years ago a lot of big commons were caught, but quite a few were killed, and so the species ran into decline. It is believed that they are a slow-growing and slow-maturing species, but the tag-and-release promotional work looks as though it has paid dividends, as the last year or two has seen commons of 70–120lb being landed. Ullapool in western Ross is a good area, renowned for the famous competitions it used to hold. Scapa Flow in the Orkney Islands has seen its share of big 'flatties', which proves the point I made earlier—this species can turn up in any situation, from shallow, minimal tide areas like the west of Ireland bays to the deep-water tidal flows of Scotland. In both cases location is the key, as once you have taken a skate from an area, perseverance in that same area should yield others.

I have received a summary of tagging results up to 1989 from the Department of Natural History at Glasgow Museum. The tags used are called dart tags, and consist of a sliver of thin plastic with a small retaining barb on the end. A 'do not kill' message and tag number are printed on the tag, and it is applied with a steel canula on the end of a pole, much like a broom handle. You simply place the dart tag in the pointed end of the canula with the barb left showing. The tag is then pushed into the fish near the trailing edge of its wing, around the location of the tail. The barb should be pushed in out of sight and the canula given half a twist and removed, leaving the tag in place. Details such as locality, depth, bait, date, sex, weight, length, width and time are marked down on the tagging card, and the results are collated by the Glasgow Museum.

The Species

While most of the skate have remained relatively local (around Mull and the Inner Hebrides), some have migrated to the west of Lewis and Northern Ireland. The tagging has also revealed that only male skate of between about 70 and 130lb are being caught, whereas females may weigh anything from 15 to 192lb. The reasons for this are not yet clear. A few fish have been caught several times, giving an indication of growth rates. The best example is a male (No. 558) originally caught in August 1978 (32lb). It was subsequently recaptured three times, in June 1985 (75lb), July 1986 (79lb) and June 1987 (116lb).

The new 'spaghetti' tags are similar to those I use myself for the NMFS in America for shark tagging. They seem to have an excellent life and durability. Glasgow Museum hopes to involve more people in tagging in the future, as angler awareness can only be good for the future of skate fishing. Although figures were uncertain at the time of going to press, it appears that there have been 250 big skate tagged to date, with 33 recaptures. There is a standard reward (currently £3) for any tag details recovered.

The two other skate that might possibly be encountered by the angler are the white skate and long-nose skate. Any big skate is rare enough for the average angler just to call it a 'common', but in fact there are differences. The white skate is likely to be the largest encountered, and it is distinguished by being almost pure white on the underbelly. It also has something of a bottle nose, which gives rise to the name bottle-nose skate, or Burton skate; it's far easier to remember it as the white skate. Some reports put the maximum size of this species as high as 500lb. Although commercial fishermen are likely to have seen the bigger specimens, I have yet to see any photographs of fish that size. The back colour is a slate grey/blue, with only the occasional partially obscured blotches. Southern Ireland, Cornwall, Devon and possibly the outskirts of the Bristol Channel would be a good place to put a big bait down for them. I suggest the pure white underbelly as being the most distinguishable mark with which to identify them.

The long-nosed skate is of course identified by its long nose. It may have a few blotches on the upper side, and it is a fairly bland grey on both underside and back. It grows to a much smaller size, and is widely distributed. I believe small skate of 60–80lb may well be long-nose skate misidentified as small commons. To further complicate matters there may even be an intermediate cross between the three, but the common skate is more likely to be the species the angler catches.

Big skate are usually only taken during the summer months, and although they obviously have some sort of migration pattern, I believe the reason is simply that the greatest numbers of anglers are fishing then. Other than for reproduction, I see no reason why a common skate in an

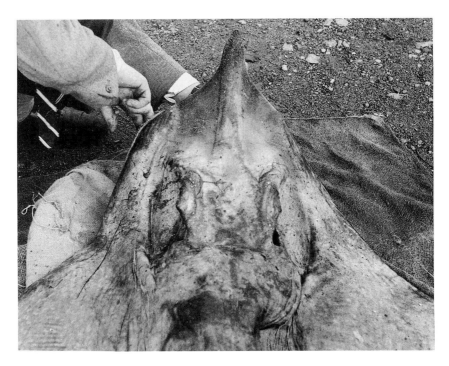

This is a close-up of a white skate of 140½lb landed from Clew Bay, although it does bear similarities to the longnose skate. (*Photo: Norman Dunlop, Central Fisheries Board*).

Irish bay should move away from what is still a fairly mild stretch of coastline. Perhaps they move to slightly deeper water but I have a feeling that they stay in the same locality much of the time. The skate is also the largest species likely to be taken from the shore—although I have yet to hook one! In Scotland it can be done, and also from Fenit Bay in Ireland. As recently as 1989 a 90-lb skate was landed by a woman fishing there from the comfort of her husband's car! I have heard of several 100-lb skate taken from the same pier, and I believe that the angler who seriously sets out to land a big common could catch one if he fished and baited the same mark over a period of time—say as little as three days.

The movements of these big skate always hold a certain fascination for me, possibly because so little is really known about them. So few have been caught, tagged and released that recapture rates are still minimal, although territoriality does ensure quite a high return from those specimens tagged. The Central Fisheries Board (CFB) in Ireland keeps records of tagged fish of many species, and has taken the common skate off their specimen fish list, since to register your fish as a specimen it has to be killed. This decision was taken in 1976, and was to last for three years, with only possible new record fish being allowed to be killed. Such was the success of the enterprise that a complete ban was introduced until further notice, with the committee reviewing the situation annually.

The CFB's leading sea-angling officer, Norman Dunlop, has provided some statistics recorded by his department. The greatest known distance ever travelled by a tagged common skate was 104 miles. This fish was tagged at Courtmacsherry, Co. Cork, in July 1978, and was recaptured in a trawl 1678 days later, west of Dingle, Co. Kerry. There was one other skate which may have travelled further, but details are sketchy. This fish was tagged at Castletownsend, Co. Cork, in August 1981 and was recaptured more than 100 miles away 'somewhere' off the south-west of Ireland by a French trawler in August 1983. An estimated distance of 120 miles in 730 days has been logged for this fish.

It is very interesting to note that out of a further nineteen recaptures, sixteen fish were found less than 35 miles from the original place of tagging. In fact eleven of these are reported to have been recaptured in exactly the same location as when first tagged. The number of days of liberty for these very localised fish ranged from 10 days to 842 days.

There has been only one white skate recapture. It was tagged at Enniscrone (Killala Bay) on 29 July 1979 and was recaptured 975 days later, just three miles away at Lackan, on 30 March 1982. As for the smaller thornback ray, the greatest distance ever travelled was 72 miles. This fish was tagged half a mile south-west of Fenit Island lighthouse, Tralee Bay, on 26 September 1983 and was recaptured in a trawl, north-west of Bull Rock, west Cork on 26 April 1984, having been at liberty for 933 days. The vast majority of some 160 recaptured thornbacks have been taken very close, sometimes within yards of the original place of tagging. The longest surviving thornback was first tagged in Tralee Bay, on 4 August 1981 when it weighed $4\frac{1}{2}$lb. It was recaptured on 5 August 1987, 28 miles away in a trawl off Blasket Sound. It weighed $14\frac{1}{2}$lb.

The Irish record halibut weighed 156lb and was caught by Frank Brogan during a competition at the Stags, Portacloy, Belmullet in July 1982. Ireland must surely have many untapped common skate, white skate and halibut marks still yet to realise their full potential. Many of the northern areas see little or no serious attempts at these big fish, and I feel sure with dedicated anglers using 50-lb stand-up tackle and large baits, some incredible fish could be taken off the Irish coast.

Thornback Skate

This is the species most likely to have been landed by the sea angler.

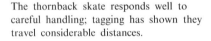

The thornback skate responds well to careful handling; tagging has shown they travel considerable distances.

Caught over the clean sand of Blacksod Bay, this thornback has less contrasting back markings due to the plain environment of the sandy seabed. Angler is Chris Kent from Birmingham. This was his first ever thornback.

Popular as a food fish and present in large numbers, it must surely be the most common catch of all the skate and ray family. Although the small-nosed rays are properly classified as rays, the thornback still retains its name as skate. Presumably this is because it appears as skate in the fish and chip shops, as it is very susceptible to the commercial trawl net. Known on the east coast as the roker, it can be caught year-round, but the greatest numbers occur during spring and summer.

They are a welcome species on a day when bites are few and far between, yet they are maligned when the angler is in pursuit of other adversaries. They have a mottled brown back, sometimes with striking black blotches and sharp thorns. These thorns can vary from individual to individual, and can cover the back right down to the tail. They are not poisonous, but care should be taken in handling and unhooking the fish.

There is a place to pinch a finger and thumb just to the side of the nose, which is safe, and gives a firm grip.

Thornback skate are good to eat, but the hassle of cleaning them puts me off keeping any but the odd one. The best meat is from the wings, and you need not worry about bones, as they are only cartilage and the cooked meat slides right off them. Winging should be done as soon as possible after capture, because if it has been in the fish box for any length of time it tends to 'slime up' on the outside, and is very unsavoury to clean. Once you have cut the wings off—and a good skipper or crew may do this for you—you should skin it as already described and then cook it. A final tip is that skate produce a strong ammonia flavour if cooked directly after capture, so you would do better to leave it in the fridge on some paper towel for at least twenty-four hours to allow this ammonia to leave the meat. Apparently it can make you sleepy if you eat it too soon after capture, but this could well be an old wives' tale.

The thornback must be a prolific breeder as they are common round our coastline. They come inshore during early spring and summer, moving into larger estuaries and bays. In deeper water close to shore they can be taken by the shore fisherman, and they represent a good catch for most beach fishermen. They have the same underslung mouth as a common skate. The difference between male and female, apart from the claspers, is that the female has flat teeth on its grinding jaws, while the male's teeth are pointed. They feed best at night. Their food consists of any immature fish, crabs, tiny lobsters, shrimps, hermit crabs and other crustaceans. They locate their prey primarily by smell and vibration, flopping down to smother it before they can locate it with the mouth.

As an average size for thornbacks around the British Isles I would suggest something in the region of 7lb. Occasionally an area will have an average into double figures, but there will of course be less fish. I once fished a sandbank in Blacksod Bay, Co. Mayo, where we had been catching pack tope in the main flood channel. The rays on the edge of the channel were only about 3 or 4lb on average, but they took baits literally within a minute of the lead hitting bottom. Generally, the greater the numbers you find, the smaller the fish.

A typical thornback mark would be over sand, sand and mud or broken shell-grit. I prefer shell-grit, as I believe they often venture on to small broken ground where the crab population is densest. They are unlikely to be caught over large rocks as this habitat prevents them from catching their prey easily. There is no way they can flop down and smother a prey if there are rocks under which the prey can escape. They like to feed on sandbanks, or in small gullies between outcrops of rocks where the food is funnelled down to them. They can flop along at a reasonable pace, but they are not equipped to chase larger baitfish free-swimming above them.

The only bait they will take avidly is the sand eel. There couldn't be anything that swims faster than a sand eel, but their habit of burying themselves under gravel banks puts them within the range of the thornback. Even the sand eel must have problems wriggling out from under the blanket of a feeding thornback. A few anglers may have noticed the way rays 'curl' inwards when held for a photograph. I believe that this is how they arch their backs and force their wings down into the sand to prevent a sand eel escaping.

Some marks have been famous for their catches of thornbacks in the past. Co. Wexford's Kilmore Quay in Ireland is one such place. Carmarthen Bay is another. The Bristol Channel also offers one of the best chances of taking a double-figure thornback from the shore. The South Wales coastline in particular can be very productive, but for the most part the marks are all low-water venues. For this reason you need to be able to cast a good distance—when the flood tide starts to push you back, your bait still needs to be fished on the clean sand. Squid and lug cocktail is a bait favoured by the shore anglers fishing here.

Thornbacks lay their eggs in similar brown pouches to commons, with long tendrils that presumably help them adhere to any debris or stones on the sea bed. Spawning may take place over several months, with the fish coming in from deep water offshore in early spring, depending on the severity of the previous winter and the water temperature. The incubation periods of the egg pouches may be several months. The colour variations of thornbacks are particularly striking, blending in with the habitat they are living over. Vast open bays of clean sand yield thornbacks with a fairly bland, dirty tan colour on the back. Yet a fish taken in the vicinity of rough ground and broken shell-grit will have black patches or striations, making it look almost like another species. The mouth is quite small but extendable, and even a 5-lb ray will have a go at a fillet of mackerel. The most successful angler will be the one who leaves the bite to develop, letting the ray get the bait well inside its mouth.

Undulate Ray

This is a species to confuse you. The undulate ray has also been called the painted ray, because of the artistic striations on its back. However, in some books the painted ray is listed separately, and has also been called the small-eyed ray! It is little wonder that the world of ray identification is so confusing!

Raja undulata actually looks like the traditional ray shape in outline. Its distribution is from the north-east Atlantic—in a line across the southern North Sea to the west coast of Ireland—right down to the Mediterranean

At 12½lb, this was one of the biggest male undulate rays ever to be caught from Tralee Bay, a hotspot for the species.

and North Africa. It likes shallow water, and for that reason it is quite common in large bays on the west coast of Ireland.

This is one of the easier rays to identify. Undulating black lines cover the grey/brown back making it look as though it has been painted. They seem to be fairly common in the east of the English Channel, although Devon and Cornwall see their share of them. The south-west coastline of Ireland with its many bays and inlets is an excellent place for them, and many specimens are caught by holiday anglers fishing these waters during the summer months. Because they scavenge on the bottom, they will fall for many baits. Mackerel, herring, squid or crab baits are good, as are large bunches of lugworm tipped with a sliver of squid. Primarily a boat-caught ray, they average about six pounds, but individual specimens can reach 14lb or more. Tralee Bay has been linked in the past with many specimen undulate ray, and doubtless other bays exist which have yet to be tried.

Fishing Techniques

There are three main ways of taking these fish when boat fishing: downtide at anchor, uptide at anchor, and drifting. They can also, of course, be taken from the shore. Special techniques apply to the large species—common skate and halibut—so I have treated these separately.

Which boat-fishing technique you use depends on the topography of the sea bed and the area's speciality. A technique that applies in one area might not work in another, even if it bears all the same characteristics. It is best to stick with local knowledge, and take it from there. If one method is productive, why waste fishing time trying something totally different? Ask the skipper first and see if he thinks your technique is worth trying.

Downtide Fishing

The traditional way of fishing for rays has always been downtide. Even on many charter boats uptiding is still not used regularly. A few specialise in it, but generally downtide fishing is still the norm. The term downtide merely means all the lines will be streaming away from the stern of the boat in the tidal current. When the anchor goes down the bow of the boat will swing into any tide flow, leaving the stern at the downstream end. When a party of anglers is on a charter boat, the angler in the stern can use the lightest lead, while the one nearest the bow will have to use the heaviest.

Occasionally all the anglers use the same weight, and one might expect all the baits to rest on the bottom, the same distance apart as the anglers standing in the boat. However, the diameters of the lines, the size of bait used and the number of hooks, swivels etc on the terminal tackle all affect how the tidal flow works on the line. An angler using a fish strip the size of an index finger, say for whiting, may be fishing in the stern with a 4oz lead. The angler at the bow might have exactly the same lead and terminal

The smile says it all. Author Graeme Pullen with a beautifully-marked thornback skate taken on the downtiding technique.

gear, but be using two large fillets of mackerel for conger. The tide pushes harder on the big bait and drags the terminal gear through the other anglers' lines. When the angler at the front gets a bite he will jerk the rod. The angler next down the line, not realising that he is crossed by the line, will see his tip jump and strike back, thinking it is a fish. This is even more likely when there is a wind across the tide. As the boat moves from side to side on the anchor rope, anglers on either side become entangled with each other. I have seen anglers striking and pumping against each other in a tangle, both thinking they have a fish! It is all very amusing until it happens to you! Anglers fishing in the stern do have the option of using a light lead and 'bouncing' their bait downtide, out of the way of the other lines. You cannot do this from the bow, as you simply bounce the bait straight into the lines of the anglers downtide of you.

The smaller rays like thornbacks use the same method of feeding as the big commons. They flop on to their prey, then shuffle about until they locate it with their mouths. For this reason you need to ensure that you stay in constant contact with your bait, fished hard on the bottom. When you get a bite you should pull off a yard or so of slack to give the fish time to take the bait properly. Premature striking only results in either missed or foul-hooked fish.

Very often the angler fishing at the uptide end of the boat catches the most ray. This is because he is using the heaviest lead to keep clear from tangling other lines, which ensures that he is in constant contact with his bait. Even if he isn't, the heavier lead is more likely to hold the bait hard on the bottom. He can bounce his bait safely away from the other lines, but he must remain in contact with the lead. To maintain contact with the bottom, which is where the rays are, follow this procedure. Take your reel out of gear, but keep your thumb on the spool. Then lift the rod very high, dragging the lead off the bottom. Once it is as high as you can get it, release the spool, letting line run off, and watch the rod tip, which will jump as the lead hits bottom. Stop the spool again with your thumb immediately that happens. Let the tide pressure build up on the line for thirty seconds, then sweep the rod up again and repeat the procedure. The lower the angle of the line against the tide, the more chance your lead has of holding bottom.

A problem arises when an angler feels the lead hit bottom, raises the rod tip to pull the lead up, lets line run off, but then fails to recognise or feel when the lead hits bottom again. He simply lets line keep peeling off the spool, and a huge belly effect is produced by the tide. This pulls on the line and the angler thinks he is still dropping to the bottom. Eventually he stops the spool anyway, and the lead is on the bottom for a while, but the angle of the line will change and the tide will push the line until the lead has planed well off the sea bed. The angler is in effect fishing midwater, where nothing is ever going to take the bait.

When you have mastered the technique of downtiding, you need to stay in contact with the lead, which can also plane off the bottom, even at a shallow angle. You should ask the skipper whether the tide is going to pick up in pace, as you will have to add more lead if you are holding bottom with a light lead on an early flood or ebb tide. Once the full bore of the tide has eased you can afford to drop down a few ounces, as the lighter the lead used to hold bottom, the more positive the bite will be.

In very strong tidal flows even standard downtiding may not keep the lead on the bottom. In that case you will have to go to wire line, which has a thinner diameter than nylon of the same breaking strain, and which allows you to 'cut' through the tidal flow and use a lighter lead. It also has no stretch and hence any bite will be transmitted up the line to your rod tip. A better method of bite detection would be hard to find. You should adopt the same technique as for standard downtiding, raising and lowering the rod to let line run back. However, wire line needs careful handling if you are to get the best from it, as it springs into coils when tension is released. As soon as the lead hits bottom, drop the reel in gear and maintain pressure with the rod top. Bites will be difficult to miss, but remember that wire line transmits every tremor and tremble. When using it, allow extra time for a ray to take the bait.

There are two types of wire line to use—single strand or cabled strands. Nicro is probably the best wire for single-strand use, but it coils angrily when it comes off the spool, and it kinks, although you can unkink it. It has a thicker diameter than cabled strand. Multi-strand wire line is finer in diameter and also has a tendency to kink, but it doesn't spring off the spool quite as easily as single strand. Kinks, however, are far harder to get out, and will part under pressure. The answer with both types of wire line is to look after them as best you can. I have had some for years, but I spray it after a freshwater washdown, using either Superlube or WD40.

I advise using wire line if you are a competent angler and want to get the best from an area of strong tide, but it means using a rod with roller guides. It is possible to use a rod fitted with just a roller tip and intermediate guides with hard inserts. This reduces friction and wear on the guides. A standard chrome ring will eventually be permanently grooved by wire line. Another tip is to use a reel with a large-diameter spool. The smaller the spool diameter, the greater the tendency to coil. Use a Penn Mariner narrow-spooled reel, which is ideally suited to the storage of wire line. They are also geared, and with a star drag are ample for any ray you are likely to take in British waters.

Only three rigs are required for ray fishing at anchor. For standard downtiding, with nylon line and medium to weak tidal conditions I use a running leger rig with two hooks on the trace, one swivel, a bead and a running boom to stop the trace tangling round the mainline on the drop down. I use two small fillets of mackerel on each hook, about four inches long and one inch wide. I have found this about the optimum size for general run-of-the-mill thornbacks. The hook I find best is the Partridge Parrot Beak design. The trace length is about six feet, with the dropper snood about midway along. This is good for other species as well, so you never get bored.

When wire-line fishing in strong tides the bait will be moving about in the current. In semi-clear waters I usually like a bait with some movement, and a long trace ensures that I get it. With rays though, you need the mackerel fillet on the bottom, so don't use a trace longer than about four feet. I use a much larger bait for this method—an entire side of mackerel split down the centre to make a long flowing bait. Hook the bait just once, certainly no more than twice, otherwise it will spin up in the current.

You can now add a flasher spoon uptrace from the hook, which will flop around in the tide and attract the rays, which will probably pick up the vibrations, as in deep water the light penetration must be minimal. You can purchase flasher spoons from many tackle shops, or you can make your own from a plastic tablespoon, cutting off the handle and drilling an eyelet near the base. Around the Isle of Wight, traces with three or four flasher spoons in a row are used for cod, but they also attract rays and skate. Spoons located a foot or more from the bait can only enhance the chance of taking a ray, and on a charter with other anglers aboard it may be the method to make the ray come to your bait.

I have also found that luminous muppets work very well in place of the flasher spoons, and they might even enhance a deep jigged bait for halibut.

Uptide Fishing

For uptiding you not only need different tackle, as described in the chapter on tackle. You also need a completely different approach to presentation. The idea is to cast your bait away from the side of the boat, well uptide, and allow the grip lead to hold it without dragging round. This technique was developed for fishing shallow water marks, generally east-coast sandbanks, where it was thought that in-boat noise and the thrumming of the anchor rope in the tide put fish off. Whether it does or not is a moot point, but the fact that several baits are spread out in a wide arc does mean that any smell lane from the boat will be wider. If a boat has a stern beam of twelve feet and all the anglers are dropping straight downtide, that smell lane will be about fourteen feet. If a couple of anglers drop downtide and others cast out from either side, the smell lane might be fifty yards across! It is small wonder that it is successful.

There is a technique to this type of fishing. First, the lead cannot hold bottom with the line held across the flow of the tide—it will simply drag round, even if you have 2lb of lead on. You need to use leads with wire grips in them, either the collapsible type that fold up when you strike or the fixed wire leads that have the wire sprouting from the nose end of the lead, allowing you to bend them round like a grapnel anchor. Cast out uptide, allow the bait to hit bottom, but then, in complete contrast to downtiding, allow a great belly of line to develop. This goes downtide of the lead, with the pressure of the tide on the line actually pulling the wires into the sand, anchoring the bait in the required position. I like to use only one setup here, a long flowing trace. The lead is anchored by the grip wires, so I don't have to worry about retaining contact with the sea bed. You'll also need a light shock leader of at least 30lb to avoid cracking off during the cast. Remember that you will be casting from the confines of the boat so be careful.

For your terminal tackle, simply slide up a grip of the required weight, either folding or fixed wires. Slide up a plastic bead, tie on a barrel swivel, then a long flowing trace at least 8ft long and a single hook. Attach your bait. You may find that the trace is hanging in the water when you go to cast. All you do to 'tidy up' your cast is lightly hook the bait on to a spike of the lead. This halves its length and is released on impact with the water. This is all you need, and when a fish takes the bait you will get confirmation on the rod tip. You then have the option of either feeding out some slack line or winding out the slack and striking.

When you are after small rays and you know you can use small baits, it's possible to get away with a paternoster tackle. The lead is tied to the link swivel on the end of the mainline, and a hook length is tied to the mainline about 4ft up from the lead. It is fixed in this position either by a loop or by a three-way swivel, and the trace is kept to about five- or six-feet long. Again a single hook with a smaller bait is dropped on to the prong of wire and consigned to the depths. The lead will hit bottom, and you should pay out line until you are happy that it has gripped. Then you are ready. When a fish takes, it will not pull line from the reel, as the trace is fixed to the mainline and not on a running leger rig. The fish will come up and take the bait, and as it goes to move off, it will hook itself against the grip lead. It will pull the grip lead free so that from your end of the rod all you will see will be a bite or two on the rod top then, after a sharp tug, everything will fall slack as the fish moves away downtide. All you need do is wind out the slack belly in the tide until you establish contact with the ray, then thump the hook in. The remaining fight is the same as for any other rig.

You can also make up a running paternoster rig, which gives something of the best of both worlds, but I think that a straight running leger and a fixed paternoster are the best two rigs to use.

Without a doubt uptiding is a very successful tactic, especially when fishing over sandbanks in shallow water but with a strong tide run. It has been proved under many situations that in those conditions, uptiding outfishes downtiding.

Drifting

Drifting is a specialised local technique, and is used when the rays are thin on the ground and you need to go searching for them, rather than waiting for them to come to you. If rays are in a particular area then you will always catch them more quickly at anchor. But drifting does search them out.

A drift depends on the area being covered and the strength of the tide and wind. You may have half an hour's drift on a calm day with a neap tide, but only fifteen minutes on a windy day with a bigger spring tide. Thirty minutes is the average drifting time and this would cover quite a big area. It should be remembered that rays are slow feeders and they are not going to take a bait dragging along at two knots. I believe that rays smell the bait first, and if the bait is only bumping along the bottom slowly, it will then see it and home in.

You must remember that their method of feeding is to flop on to the prey, smothering it with their wings, then to locate it with the mouth. At anchor you should have no problems, providing you give them some slack line. When drifting, however, many anglers make the mistake of keeping the reel in gear. I do exactly the opposite. I drop the bait to the bottom, and when the lead hits I let more line peel from the spool slowly. Instead of the line being vertical, it slants down at an angle. If I feel a take I can release my thumb from the spool immediately, letting the ray take the bait completely unhindered. It may take some time to distinguish between a bite and the lead catching bottom, so if you are in any doubt let some line slack to the fish. If the lead or terminal tackle becomes snagged, try bouncing it out before you decide to pull for a break.

On a fast-drifting boat over patchy broken ground, I don't advise the use of wire line. It can be good for bite detection, but I feel it is more suited to fishing at anchor. It's ideal for fishing over sandy ground, but over boulders it might get snagged, which could prove expensive. The only way to use wire line over rough ground is to fish with a rubbing leader of 30-lb line or less, about 20ft long. When you thread your loop of wire through the rod rings, attach a split ring, then the snap swivel. Make up your terminal gear exactly as you would normally, but leave about fifteen feet from the Clement's boom, up towards the rod top and the wire line. Then if you become snagged and pull for a break, the 30-lb line should break before anything else. Breaking out wire line is no fun, it can be dangerous to unguarded fingers, and it is expensive. Better to lose a short length of rubbing leader, than half a spool of expensive wire! The other problem with wire on the drift is that when you become snagged, the non-stretch qualities of the material prevent you from using any elasticity to 'bounce' your lead free from the snag.

But if you can get used to drift fishing with wire, you can actually feel what sort of ground you are drifting over by raising the rod top, then lowering it to bump the lead on the bottom. You can tell whether you are over sand, broken ground or hard, flat rock. You'll also feel when the rays flop on the bait, so keep the reel out of gear with your thumb on the spool, ready to give line the instant a ray takes.

I like to use a two-hook trace for my drifting, and tend to use small- to medium-sized baits. Much depends on how fast the drift is. A ray has more chance of getting a small bait into its mouth than a large fillet of mackerel. I like to rely on both smell and visual stimulants. Anointing a bait with a liberal coating of either pilchard oil or Berkley Strike does no harm, and may encourage a passing ray to move in the direction of your dragged bait.

For visual attraction you have three methods. Flasher spoons work well, especially on a fast drift, when the spoons catch the current and revolve or tumble well. You could also try a luminous squid head, similar to the plastic muppets you can buy. They glow, and definitely do not put rays off. I have caught many rays while using them. Finally, you could try attaching a Cyalume chemical lightstick about two feet uptrace from the hook. These are small plastic phials containing two different chemicals. You bend the phial to crack the internal one, and when the chemicals mix the whole lightstick glows brightly. In warm weather they are brighter, but glow for a shorter period than in the cold. If you use a twelve-hour green lightstick—the most successful for me—they can be stored in the freezer and used at a later date. You could actually use a large lightstick for two trips. You can use any of these methods, or all three.

When drifting, remember that any fish will feel heavier than it really is as you drag it through the water. Take your time playing it out, especially if you are on light tackle. Should you run across a good piece of ground any skipper worth his salt will make a mental note of any landmarks. Most drifting covers a wide area, much of which will be like desert, especially on clean sand which will have been scraped barren by the trawlers. The best areas are those with fringes of rough and rocks, just enough to put the trawlers off. There is little point in drifting the barren areas of ground twice, so if the skipper has any difficulty finding the marks, drop over a 1-lb lead attached to 12-lb line and tie a fully blown balloon on to the other end. Leave 20ft of slack for tidal pull, and you should be able to see where the mark is for a second drift.

Sometimes after a single drift the skipper will steam back up the same line to drift through the area again. Ask him to move thirty yards either side on each drift, so that you are covering a different piece of ground. Remember that you are out to find the fish, rather than letting them come to you. On a pleasant sunny day with the water sparkling, nothing is more satisfying than to doze off with your feet on the gunwale waiting for a skate or ray to flop on the bait. On a rain-swept morning in a gale, with the boat rolling like a pig, you may wish you were back in home, and hope never to see a fish again. Such is fishing!

Shore Fishing

On the shore, there are two areas to try for skate and rays: from rocks or from the beach. A plain open surf beach is not the sort of place you would usually expect to find rays, however, as they dislike the pounding surf, and seem to like some depth over their backs. Rock fishing is likely to yield the best results, particularly where the rocks drop away into deep water and

the ground is clean sand, or shell-grit. A little tidal flow is even better.

The thornback skate is possibly the most popular species to take from the shore, but the best scrappers are the small-eyed rays, or the blonds. Most of the other species are boat-caught fish. For thornbacks from the rocks, the best baits I have found are mackerel soused with pilchard oil, or even better, a cocktail of squid and lugworm. The latter bait is particularly good for taking double-figure thornbacks in and around the Bristol Channel area. For the small-eyed ray and the blond ray, live or dead sand eel is the best bait, with peeler crab coming in a close second. For thornback fishing from the rocks, the west coast of Ireland takes some beating. I once fished a mark from Clifden, and in an afternoon and a day, three of us landed an incredible seventeen thornbacks. As is usually the case in Ireland, most of those were small—up to 6lb, but the sheer number of bites made it seem as though we were having the best ray fishing in the world. Night fishing from such marks would be even more successful, but all the seventeen thornbacks we took came during daylight hours.

This particular mark was a short rocky headland jutting out into a long narrow bay. I wouldn't class it as an estuary, as only a small river emptied into it. I believe the rays move into such areas to feed on the crab population, mostly in the summer and autumn. The other reason for the high numbers in such areas of course could be that the trawlers cannot work in such confined bays and inlets, leaving the ray population relatively

Previous page, left: When access is difficult, always get your fishing partner to climb down the rocks to lift out your fish. Never fish rocky headlands alone, and beware of a heavy swell on rough days.

Previous page, right: Piers offer the chance for the angler to place his bait in deep water. This Welsh angler landed a 7-lb thornback on mackerel strip.

These anglers are tackling up to fish an early flood tide in the evening from the famed Monknash Point in South Wales. The venue is a low water mark that produces rays to peeler crab and fresh sandeel.

undisturbed. They also move inshore generally around the spring for spawning, but they are present in greatest numbers when crab populations are high. You would think then that peeler crab would be the first choice of bait, but the resident crabs simply strip the soft peeler from the hook in minutes. You need a tough bait like mackerel strip tied with the flesh inwards using a binding of elasticated cotton. The outer skin of the mackerel keeps the crabs at bay for a bit longer. Squid is a good choice, and tipped with lugworm it could be the best ray bait.

The small-eyed and blond rays tends to be caught mostly off Devon and Cornwall where shore anglers have access to very deep water and strong tidal flows from the many headlands and spits of rock. If I had to make a choice, I would recommend the north Cornish and north Devon coast rather than the south. This is because of the freshwater influence of the River Severn running into the Bristol Channel. The entire channel area seems to be something of a nursery for small fish, and perhaps the small-eyed rays come in here to breed. The water in the east of the Bristol Channel is always a murky colour, and this helps fish to feed confidently through the daylight hours. Again, night is better, but even bright days in high summer offer the chance of a ray. A top mark for small-eyed ray is around Trevose Head. This famous shore mark has produced many specimen fish and must be ranked alongside Foreland Point as a great shore area for all species of fish.

Over on the South Wales coast much of the rock extends well out to the low-water mark. In high water, your lead is liable to land in rocks or kelp, so the area should be approached as a low-water, night-session mark. There are fewer deep-water cliff marks to fish from here.

There must be many good ray marks yet to be discovered by shore anglers, not from the point of view of accessibility, but from the approach adopted. You need to set out your stall very much with skate and ray in mind, and anglers fishing rock marks in summer either use lures or floatfish or put out worm baits for anything that comes along. You should really concentrate on putting out a big bait as far as you can, and patiently sitting there for several hours.

My favourite method is the running paternoster with a collapsible grip lead. You need a shock leader of about 40lb, as you will need to give a big bait plenty of power for a good cast. The grip lead ensures your bait is held in the one position in a strong tide and a running paternoster, as opposed to a fixed paternoster, lets you feed slack line to a taking fish without their feeling any resistance. My experience is that in strong currents the ray moves up to a bait, picks it up then drifts back downtide slowly as it tries to eat it. If you use a fixed paternoster it cannot drift back, and while there is a chance it will hook itself against the grip lead, I think there is an equal chance it might spook and drop the bait if it feels any unnatural resistance.

Scent must play an important part in shore fishing, and I use a mixture of pilchard oil and sodium laurel sulphate. Pilchard oil floats, and it rises from the bottom through the water currents. Sodium laurel sulphate is an emulsifying agent which ensures that the oil stays near the sea bed. Although it can only be bought at a chemist's, you can also try the other emulsifiers that can now be purchased in tackle shops, mainly for carp fishermen. They are a lot quicker than sodium laurel sulphate, and more convenient to use. This mixture is good when used on mackerel for thornback skate.

For small-eyed ray and blond ray live sand eel is surely the best bait. They hunt faster than the thornback and frequent areas of stronger tide, which are also the habitat of sand eels. Live sand eels need to be cast carefully, and you should opt for a venue that allows you to cast without smashing them by hard casting pressure. You can also use dead sand eels. They are not quite as good, but they certainly account for a good number of shore-caught rays—possibly the vast majority, as keeping sand eels live is a problem in itself. Another good tip is to use an entire fillet of launce or greater sand eel. These can sometimes be taken from deep-water marks while you are feathering for mackerel. They can actually be taken by design if you take the trouble to tie up miniature sets of launce feathers. They are too large on their own, but a long side fillet, hooked just a couple of times then bound to the hookshank with elasticated thread, looks something like a sand eel.

When the tide flow is slower or you have a period of slack tide, even on a big spring, you can opt to roll a plain lead around rather than anchor a bait with the grip lead. Remember that the blonds and small-eyed rays are possibly more fish-orientated and will therefore respond well to a slowly moving bait. Make sure that you change your terminal rig to a running leger, using a bait clip up the trace to stop the bait breaking up on the cast. Also make sure that you use a bomb with a barrel swivel incorporated in it—either a lead with a swivel melted into its body or a link swivel which can be clipped to the standard lead loop. The reason for this is to prevent any rolling lead from twisting the trace and hook around the mainline. You want the strip of launce to look as natural as possible, and a rolling lead with a trace about 4–5 ft long will allow just that.

If you are fishing with peeler crab over an area of clean ground in front of you, make your first cast count. Get the crab out as far as you can and leave it there for at least twenty minutes, then reel in to check whether other crabs have stripped the hook clean. If they have, don't leave the peeler crab in the water for quite so long. There is no point in sitting there with a bare hook! Another tip is to avoid using fine elasticated thread for binding the peeler to the hook. This can be pulled too tight, cutting into the meat and letting those all-important juices seep out too quickly. The beauty of peeler crab is that the juices send the fish on a feeding spree, so use thick elasticated thread and bind it gently, because the thread itself will then soak up some of the juices. The more smell you have in the water around the hook, the better your chances of success.

Squid and lugworm are a favourite cocktail of mine for thornbacks, but you should put the hook once through the top end of a sliver of squid, then thread a lugworm up the shank and follow up by nicking the tail end of the squid sliver on to the hook. That holds the lugworm on comfortably and prevents it flying off during the cast. You will also have to bind the top end of the squid sliver to the hook eye or main trace to prevent it sliding round the bend and bunching up on the bottom. If you want to use squid alone, just put the head on, leaving the tentacles trailing enticingly in the current. There are occasions when lugworm on its own is successful, but I emphasise the need to pile on three or four worms to make a good mouthful. When using squid on its own, I cover it with pilchard oil and emulsifier. When using a cocktail of squid and lug, or lug on its own, do not put on any additives. Like peeler crab, lugworm have their own important body juices, with amino acids high on the list. This is a proven fish attractor, so don't taint what is an important smell by using an additive that might not be as good.

Herring can be a good bait, either used whole on boat-fishing trips or filleted from the shore. Bind it well with elasticated thread if you are distance casting or uptiding. Sprats are occasionally productive, but I don't rate them very highly for rays. King ragworm is a definite catcher when shore fishing, and comes into its own when fished near a fringe of rocks with a little tide, bordering on to an open shell-grit beach. If you cannot get king ragworm, just pile on two or three ordinary ragworms, and try spraying them with Berkley Strike fish additive—it seems to work quite well. They also work better on a rolling lever rig and plain bomb as described above, in small-movement tidal conditions.

Techniques for Common Skate and Halibut

When it comes to methods for finding either big common skate or the elusive halibut you should think big. These fish don't grow large by eating just the odd crab. Their diet also consists of small fish. For that reason I advise the use of whole-fish baits like mackerel, pollock or coalfish. Top of the list must come a 2-lb mackerel. Obviously freshly caught fish are better than frozen, but even a frozen bait, liberally coated with pilchard oil, will still take fish.

Common skate are a slow species, and as I have said, their *modus operandi* must be to trap small fish and crabs under their ample wings, then shuffle about until they can crunch the prey up in their teeth. This method of feeding often gives rise to some big fish being lost by inexperienced anglers through inadvertent foulhooking.

The skate lumbers along and picks up the smell from the bait, but as it homes in the wings hit the vertical line up to the rod. The angler gets a sharp jolt on the rod tip, thinks it is a bite, and thumps the hook straight into the skate's wing. I have explained the difficulty in getting skate up from the bottom, but a foulhooked common skate in a strong tide flow gives all the pulling power of a runaway train. It is small wonder that broken lines are blamed on big halibut or porbeagle sharks.

Once you get that initial bump on the line, pay out some slack so that the line lies flat and the skate can snuffle around until it gets the bait in its mouth. Even then you may get some strange vibrations tingling up the line. My belief is that the skate is crushing the bait in its teeth at this stage. Restrain the urge to strike, and wait until the line is pulling from the reel at a steady rate. Then all you need do is engage the reel, wind out the slack and thump the hook home.

Many anglers fish with a pre-tested drag that they associate with a fast-moving fish. I like to fish with the drag pretty well locked up. After all the skate is on the bottom–it can't crash dive any further, and the most important factor in making the battle short is to apply the absolute maximum pressure as soon as you set the hook. If you simply strike and have a low drag setting on the reel, the skate will be suctioned on the bottom by the time you drop the rod top to pump it. Hit it hard, then without dropping for another pump hang on with both hands and hold the pressure on until the rod starts to lift. Crank and pump as quickly as possible so that it never has any let-up from the pressure. Then once it is off the bottom, ease the drag a touch and take your time. Unless there is a strong tidal flow, the fish will be yours. Most of the marathon battles with skate occur when the angler fails to get them off the bottom, and spends half an hour with the rod bent over and nothing happening.

The only other danger period with common skate is near the boat. They may change direction at the last moment as the tide catches their wings, so be prepared for the sudden increase in pressure, and tell the boatman to release the trace rather than clinging tight and breaking the fish off. Once off the bottom, the skate should be yours providing you keep up the pressure. This initial power surge of the rod at hooking stages is the reason I think the American style of stand-up rods would be ideally suited to skate fishing. Once you have taken the stretch out of the line and struck the hook home, the rod can apply immense pressure to the fish without hurting the angler. Hold that pressure and gain line with short pumps, and you could see the skate record tumbling in very short order. It remains to be seen if anglers will catch on to the fact that the new stand-up rod blanks are totally different in design from anything else they may have used, but for skate, halibut and shark, they are surely the British angler's tool of the future.

The sort of equipment required to take big skate and halibut is dealt with in the chapter on tackle, but I feel I should emphasise the need to keep your bait on the bottom at all times. Wire line is good for keeping contact with your lead, and in fact you can use less weight with it, as the thinner diameter cuts through the tide flow better. However I feel it is not really practical to use wire with big fish. To keep that bait hard on the bottom dispense with all ideas of paternoster booms or small 'flyer' hooks with small baits up the line for bonus small fish. Chances are you will be winding up a small fish just at the time a big common skate is homing in to the smell of your bait! If you are fishing for big skate use a long flowing trace, a large single hook and a big bait. It's as simple as that. You need a Clement's boom or something similar, so that a taking fish doesn't feel the drag of the lead. I don't think they drop the bait because they fear something is amiss. I think they move off, and the lead pulls or stops the bait from being taken in their mouth as they move around.

The basic setup would be to slide a boom of your choice up the mainline, following it with a bead. Then you should tie the mainline to a trace you have made up at home. My tip for a trace would be at least 6ft, sometimes 8ft, of heavy-duty nylon monofilament, at least 130lb in breaking strain. The skate may scuff it up, but it doesn't possess the cutting teeth to slice through it. To one end of the trace attach a large Berkley swivel, to the other a large hook like the Z22 Partridge long shank in 9/0 size. Attach your required lead, bait up and lower away. I also suggest that you put on enough lead to keep the bait on the bottom as near vertical as possible. Unlike other species, with common skate you don't want to bounce the lead continually downtide. Put it down and leave it for a fish to find. Whether you are after common, white or long-nose skate, the same setup will suffice.

If halibut are your quarry, the chances are that you will be drifting, rather than anchored as you would be for big skate. As I have said, the halibut is a far more active fish, and while taking lobster and crab on the bottom it is far more predatory and will flash up to grab live fish swimming just off the bottom. Now you need to add movement to your fishing, and be constantly in touch with your lead and bait at all times. The preferred ground will be sand or shell-grit and broken ground. One second your lead could be bumping quietly over clean ground, and the next hung in the bottom. I would also advise using 50-lb tackle, which is no fun to try and break out when it snags on the sea bed. From a fast-drifting boat you could experience some problems.

If you decide to fish a whole bait like mackerel, pollock or coalfish, I would advise you to use exactly the same setup as for the skate, but shorten that trace length to around 3ft. That way if you wind the lead a few feet off the bottom to clear snags, the bait will be close behind it. If the trace is too long, the lead may be clear but the hook and bait can still snag. By all means let the lead bounce occasionally on the bottom, but wind it up a few feet when you feel it start to hit rock. If you do feel the hook or lead snag don't immediately pull into it. Slacken off quickly, let a couple of yards of line into the water, lock up the reel and then jig it violently. Sometimes you can bounce the lead or hook out of the snag.

When you know you are fishing over clean ground, a good tip for halibut fishing is to put a flasher spoon in the terminal tackle. There are two ways to do this. You can put one about a foot or so away from the bait, but no farther. The reason for this is that the halibut will come for anything flashing in the water. If it sees and takes the bait instead, well and good. But there might be occasions when it goes for the flash of the spoon instead. By putting the flasher spoon on the trace close to the bait, the chances are good that it will take in both at the same time. If you put the spoon too far away from the hook, the halibut has nothing to hook up on. If you must put the spoon somewhere else, attach it above the boom, on the mainline, about 3ft off the bottom. This may draw fish better than a spoon near the bait. One of the best ideas is to put the spoon right above the bait, so that the flash of metal and the silver of the bait merge into one.

Keep drawing the bait up off the bottom slowly and dropping it down again to make the blade of the spoon work.

Another method that does not appear to be used much is to make up an outsize pirk. It doesn't have to be heavy for its size. In fact it should only carry enough lead to get the lure down deep. An outsize, triple-strength Mustad treble hook should be wired on to the end of the pirk. Do not use split rings, which might open up under pressure. Keep the shape of the pirk broad and flat, so that it can be jigged and flashed just off the bottom. To spice it up add a coalfish fillet to each of the treble hooks. From the eye of the pirk attach about 6ft of 130-lb test nylon, and spend the day jigging it gently. This method more than any other should be the best way to get a take from a halibut, especially over the rocky ground which they hunt over. The halibut is unlikely to bury itself in the bottom, especially over rocks, so keep the drag tight, but not too tight. Halibut are much faster moving than skate, and can strip line from a reel with fast, powerful lunges. I have devised a rig for bottom fishing with a live mackerel for deep-water porbeagle shark, incorporating about 3ft of stainless wire to make a long boom keeping the bait from swimming around the mainline. I believe this could be used to good effect by halibut anglers. From a drifting boat you need to liphook the mackerel, but from an anchored boat you can just nick the hook through the back. This is a relatively new paternoster method that is still in the experimental stage, but is very simple to make up, and cheap as well.

As I have already mentioned, Scotland has made a name for itself with the regular capture of big skate. The specialists in this line of fishing are without a doubt Duncan and Brian Swinbanks. They are based at Tobermory on the Isle of Mull, and probably have more experience than anyone in catching this unusual flatfish. I decided to contact Duncan, and he very kindly gave me permission to use some of his hard-earned information in this book. Duncan runs the tackle shop while his brother Brian is owner/skipper of the *Laurenca*. They are both joint directors of the firm Knotless Fishing Tackle Ltd, which provided anglers with a revolutionary new sea boom system that will help them to fish more efficiently.

It is the 'flying' motion of the skate, using its wings, coupled with the large body surface area that makes getting one off the bottom such a tough job. The brothers favour a fishing ground of shingle interspersed with rough ridges and boulders. They also report that the big skate like to feed very close to underwater cliffs, with angling depths of 150–250ft. When the tide flows strongly up in their area the skate tend to lie motionless. They have noted that the best time for takes is when the tide eases at slack water. On the bigger spring tides, slack water is essential as the full bore of that huge volume of water is too much for the anglers. As I have said, you must ensure that your bait is legered hard on the bottom. During periods

Common skate, and even halibut like to feed in deep water gullies with plenty of tide. With some rocks nearby, the angler has a chance of hooking a big fish.

of neap tide, however, there is always the chance of a take when the tide is running, just as long as you have your bait on the bottom.

As the current eases, the big skate set off to patrol a fairly well-defined territory. One tagged Isle of Mull fish has been caught in exactly the same place three times. The Scottish fish will often feed in groups, following the scent trails. I have noticed myself that the Irish skippers always think there is a good chance of a second fish if you had just landed one. Their opinion is that the big skate travel in pairs. Having a hook up on three different 100-lb skate at the same time can cause havoc to the nervous system of the anglers concerned! Duncan and Brian feel that when the 'prey' is encountered by the skate it is smothered by a lightning-fast pounce which produces a strong, sharp pull on the angler's rod top. This confirms my own opinion about the stingray's method of feeding from watching fish feed in the shallow water of the Florida flats. The bait is manoeuvred by feel until it is consigned to the mouth. Premature striking causes a foulhooked fish, and as these big commons are difficult enough to move off the bottom in normal circumstances, they can prove almost impossible when foulhooked. In strong tidal conditions they can plane away at an angle and be hard if not impossible to stop. I believe that reports of the 'monsters that got away' are often wing-hooked skate.

The teeth of the skate are flattened rows of crushing plates, and the Swinbanks brothers feel that a short wire trace of approximately 120-lb test is essential. This is attached to a strong swivel above which a boom and lead are free-running on the mainline. Hooks should be at least as big as a 10/0, and baited with a whole small coalfish or mackerel. They have found only one solution to the dreaded dogfish population—having a regular bait inspection. Their most productive results are obtained by playing a waiting game on a suitable mark. The 1989 season produced the best two days' fishing they had ever known. An amazing twelve skate were caught on the first day, followed by a further ten the following day.

Areas such as the Isle of Mull, Orkney, Shetland and Ullapool are famous for 100-lb-plus skate. Unfortunately Shetland and Ullapool have suffered considerably from overfishing. In Ullapool the early anglers were to blame, in Shetland the commercial long-liners. There have recently been signs of a recovery in skate stocks around Ullapool however. The record skate used to be a specimen of $226\frac{1}{2}$lb caught by Robin Macpherson from Whalesay Island, Shetland, but Brian Swinbanks achieved one of his lifetime ambitions when in July 1986 he weighed in a monster specimen skate of 227lb for angler Reg Banks. The record fish was returned alive after weighing and photographing, a triumph for conservation and a tribute to the farsightedness of the British Record Rod-Caught Committee.

This fish was by no means the biggest caught, as local long-line fishermen have taken several fish in excess of 300lb. The brothers have found that by retaining a good relationship with commercial fishermen, they can ensure that these valuable but economically worthless fish are now returned alive to the water. I also found this to be the case with several Irish skippers who, while netting in Courtmacsherry Bay, have boated and released big skate in excess of 150lb.

Over the years the Swinbanks brothers have landed these massive fish on almost every grade of tackle, from light 20-lb outfits right up to 80lb. Reasonably heavy tackle is by far the best. They advise at least a 50-lb class rod with a 4/0 multiplier, loaded with 50-lb monofilament line of a low-stretch brand. Braided lines are totally unsuitable and soon get frayed on the rocks. The skate has no swim bladder and thus do not suffer unduly from rapid changes in depth. This allows them to fight hard all the way to the surface.

All their fish are tagged and returned alive as part of a tag-and-release programme sponsored by the Angling Foundation and Knotless Fishing Tackle Ltd, in conjunction with the Glasgow Museum of Natural History.

Skate should be returned as quickly as possible, and under no circum-stances should they be lifted or weighed by the mouth. This is a delicate mechanism which can easily be damaged. The brothers are trying to have the common skate declared a protected species, which can be fished for only with rod and line and must be released.

An interesting point is that the brothers have never found long-nosed or white skate in their area. They do know of records from other fisheries where long-nosed skate are caught regularly, such as off Barra. They also find it interesting to note that many of the so-called common skate caught off Ireland are in fact white skate. These observations lead them to believe that white skate are relatively common around the Tralee Bay area in Co. Kerry. Of the elusive halibut, the only specimen they have seen while skate fishing was 56lb.

Baits

As with all fishing, each species has a preference for certain types of tackle presentation and certain baits. This seems to have little relevance to whether they normally find a particular bait in their natural habitat or not. For instance, rays and skate are highly unlikely to come across mackerel in a live state, let alone be able to catch them, yet they will take a mackerel bait. I believe they have highly developed scent buds that can be used to smell out the crustaceans and small fish like sand eels that actually live on or near the bottom. To me, sand eels have no apparent smell at all, yet the rays seem to be able to locate them under the gravel or shell-grit in a fast tide race. I assume that they must come across dead fish occasionally, and like most species will take the opportunity to scavenge what they can. The mackerel, being related to the tuna, does have a high blood content, and a fresh fillet of mackerel lying on the bottom must leave more of a smell lane than an unharmed sand eel!

Mackerel

Mackerel can be fished whole for big common skate or halibut. I still smother a whole mackerel bait in pilchard oil, or any other additive that takes my fancy. A freshly feathered mackerel is far better than frozen bait. For big commons I feel it is worth spending some time trying to get fresh bait. You may have to wait a long time for a take from a big fish, so you may as well do so with a decent bait on the sea bed.

Herring

This is a good bait for halibut, as there is plenty of flash from the silver scales. Buy them fresh from a trawler if possible, but failing that choose only the freshest from the fishmonger's slab. Avoid any that have broken

For the shore fisherman, this three hook paternoster baited with mackerel strips is ideal for locating small thornbacks.

Left: A final flurry at the boatside and another ray is caught. This fish fell to a strip of mackerel.

stomachs, as they have been frozen more than once and will probably soon break up or be nibbled away by smaller fish.

Coalfish

This is not a good visual bait because of its dark colour, but is nevertheless effective when used in an area where they are an accepted food item, such as Scotland. You can fish them whole, or remove the backbone to make a split-tail bait. Their cousin the pollock is nowhere near as good. Use fish up to 2lb if you are 'going for bear'.

Squid

Squid is a great bait from shore or boat for the thornback, small-eyed and blond rays. When boat-fishing deep water and fast tide runs use the calamari squid fished whole. When shore fishing all you need is a strip, perhaps tipping it off with a couple of lugworms. Always try squid on its own before you put on any oil-based additives. Personally the only time I can smell squid is when it has gone off—and then you can't get the taint off your fingers.

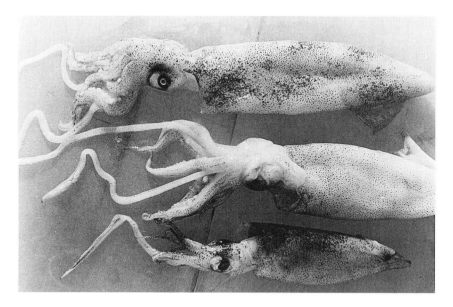

For the larger specimens, never be wary of using a big bait like these whole calamari squid. Threaded onto the hook so the head and tentacles hang downtide, they make an excellent bait.

Lugworm

Used primarily as a shore bait, you need to pile several lugworms on to the hook to get a bait large enough to provoke interest from a ray. They are better used as a cocktail with other baits.

Ragworm

Smaller ragworms are hardly worth using when you are after ray, but the larger king ragworms certainly are. They fish well for stingrays off the Essex coast or in the Solent in early summer, and for big thornbacks moving into the Bristol Channel in spring. Many shops will not stock them, and a good supply area is usually a closely guarded secret.

Crabs

These are possibly the best all-round species bait when shore fishing. You need the green shore crab in the shell-peeling stage, but if you find an edible peeler, use that as well. Use a large bait and tie it to the hook using thick elasticated thread not thin, as the latter cuts into the crab meat and lets the important juices escape. Crabs can be kept a long time if they are kept damp and cool. Frozen peeler is a good standby, but nothing can beat a fresh bait. Try fishing two rods, with frozen peeler on one rod and fresh on the other. You should find a marked difference in bites.

Mussels

This is a little-used bait for ray fishing, yet it can be good if you prepare it correctly. After collecting a large bucket of mussels at low water, shell about two dozen, then roll them in dry salt on a newspaper. This takes up any excess moisture and toughens them a bit. Work several onto the hook, but take time to bind them gently with elasticated thread. Like the peeler crab, they have important juices which you want in the water, not dripping into your wellies! Make your cast carefully, ensuring that the bulk of the bait doesn't fly off on the cast. Mussels are soft, and you should forget any thoughts of long-distance power casts. If more anglers used mussels, especially at traditional ray marks from rocks into deep water, a good deal more would be caught.

Cuttlefish

Difficult to obtain, cuttlefish are an ideal strip bait when drift fishing for smaller rays. They are particularly good when used on a long flowing trace. The tough meat is a safeguard against the attention of crabs and small fish, and it must have a smell similar to squid—it certainly does when you leave it in the garage for a week!

Razorfish

This can be a good ray bait from the shore, but I wouldn't class it as easy to obtain, and you can get so much more in the way of other species by using this valuable bait. Opportunist scavengers that they are, skates and rays will obviously eat razorfish, and must surely come across them in their normal feeding patterns, but it doesn't seem viable to thread six razorfish up the line just to make a big ray bait. If you can afford it, use them.

Sand Eels

Other baits will take rays, but surely sand eel must be the best of all. A fillet from the launce, or greater sand eel, or better still a fresh sand eel, has every chance of being taken from both boat and shore. Together with crabs, they are the most likely sources of food for the bottom-feeding skates and rays.

A super bag of thornbacks for these happy anglers. Conservation is going to play an important part in the future of sea angling, and tagging research has shown the species can survive to be recaptured.

Top shore guide, Ed Schlifkke, shows off an enormous 11-lb-plus, shore-caught, small-eyed ray. Ed runs a professional guide service from his base at St Merryn in Cornwall and has landed many big small-eye rays with his specialised techniques.

The author displays a good blond ray taken on mackerel strip from sandbanks off Jersey in the Channel Islands.

Large common skate can be weighed aboard the boat, tagged, then returned alive. (*Photo Duncan Swinbanks.*)

With a favoured habitat of clean ground, the smaller skate and rays are susceptible to trawler nets. From the angler's viewpoint, a venue that offers a proximity of rock could offer better sport.

Right: The author's stingray planes in the fast tide. In British waters, king ragworm would seem to be the best bait for stingrays in the summer months.

Facing page: Essex angler, Mick Redding, looks delighted with his first ray of the day. Mick uses freshwater carp tackle to get the best sport from his ray fishing.

Below: The eyes of the ray or skate are located on the top of the body. They catch their prey by smell, then smother it beneath their expansive wings until they can get the food into their mouth. Here you can see how difficult identification can be with just three species: a spotted ray, a small-eyed ray and a thornback skate.

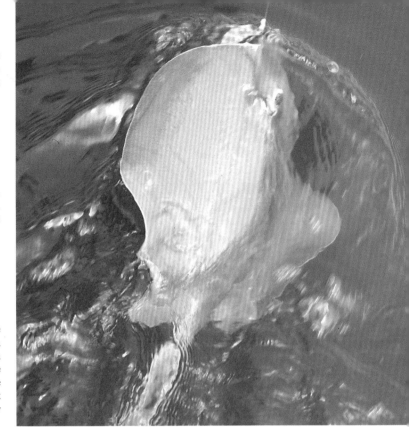

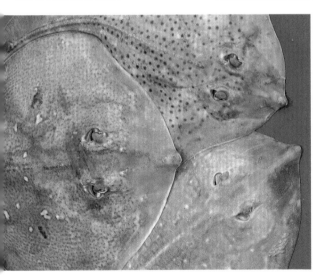

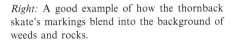

Right: A good example of how the thornback skate's markings blend into the background of weeds and rocks.

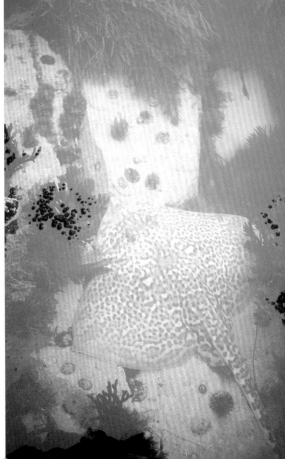

Skate and rays are nocturnal and better catches can be expected then, especially by shore anglers.

An angler fishes the uptide technique for blond ray from a Jersey sandbank. Standing on the bow ensures he can cast away from the other anglers' lines.

Two double-figure, small-eye rays that were taken using the uptide techniques from the *Joseph-Marie 2*, out of Minehead, Somerset.

Tackle

Skate and rays are both species which should be approached with tackle that will enable you to get the maximum amount of sport from them. The big boys like common and white skate, and especially halibut, require specialised tackle, as the sheer bulk of the fish requires substantial equipment. The smaller species can be taken on any gear, but to maximise your sport you should choose your outfit carefully. I see no reason to outgun your opponent completely with tackle more suited to moving furniture. A balance should be struck between a need to catch the fish, existing fishing conditions and a good bent rod.

Stand-Up Tackle

Let's look at the 'heavy' end of the market first. There is a wave of interest in a new outfit and technique called stand-up fishing. It was first introduced by the long-range charter boats operating out of ports like San Diego on the west coast of the United States. These big boats might carry a couple of dozen anglers on long-range fishing sorties down south to the fish-rich waters of Mexico and beyond. They trolled lures a lot in between travelling, and these lures were intercepted by yellowfin tuna—very large yellowfin tuna in fact. The boats might be getting multiple hookups, and with nowhere to sit down the anglers obviously lost a lot of fish.

A new range of tackle was devised by manufacturers to enable anglers hooking the yellowfins to put more pressure on the fish while still in a standing position. The rods were short, with flexible tips and incredible backbone after the first 15inches or so. This was fine, but the power simply transmitted itself to the angler's shoulders and back. The rod would hold up but the angler couldn't. New harness systems were devised, with a flat butt pad across the thighs and a shoulder harness that spread the load across the whole of the back rather than the top of the shoulders. The reels

Go Fishing for Skate & Rays

A 60-lb-plus stingray on, and the author uses a standup rod clipped to a Sampo shoulder harness and butt-pad to apply pressure. Note how you can lean back with such an outfit. Pressure is on the legs instead of lower back.

were pretty much the same, but geared reels offering two speeds are now becoming popular. The best two makes are either Penn International or Shimano. For skate and rays there is no need to change over to two-speed multiplier reels, but there could be a place for stand-up rods and the principal techniques of stand-up fishing in the common skate and halibut world.

Most British charter boats have no fighting chair for big fish, and all fish fighting is done from the standing position. Restricting the power dives of a big halibut or prising a common skate from the sea bed would be far easier with the powerful new stand-up rods. For this type of fishing I thoroughly recommend trying one, as you can still use it with a light-weight Sampo shoulder harness (providing your reel is fitted with the reel lugs to put the clips), and a regular butt pad. The butts on these rods are short, and they are light to hold. The sensitive tips will also respond well to bites, although they certainly weren't designed for this job.

Some of the skate fishing in Scotland demands heavy leads and the short sticks make pumping both lead and fish up comparatively pleasant. Penn reels are something of a household name in America, and their stand-up range of rods is about as competitive as you would need. Today, more companies are offering carbon, boron and kevlar etc as rod inclusion materials, but the Penn range seems to be as good as you are ever going to need on British species.

The tuna stick rods are quite short—5ft 6ins and 6ft—with three basic styles. Three rods, the International models 2255 AR, 2260 AR, and 2160 ARB all have Aftco roller guides throughout. For extra leverage on bigger fish, the 2160 ARB features a detachable curved Unibutt. On models 2155 USG and 3955 RCS the heavy duty Fuji braced USG silicon carbide guides give plenty of wear and tear without damaging your line. All rods feature P450 Superglass. To match up you can use the new Penn 320 GTI Super level wind multiplier featuring the HT100 drag material. I see no real need for a lever drag reel, as you are not going to be fighting a really fast-moving fish that demands critical drag settings. You need a workhorse reel, and with both hands on the rod and reel, using maximum power to lever a big common skate from the bottom, the last thing you will worry about is line lay. With the level wind the reel does it for you. Alternatively go to the Penn Senator star drag reels. The 6/0 size is about right for the job. Made from one-piece machined chrome-plated bronze spool, with easy access drag and a gear ratio of 2.1 to 1, it is 'gutsy' enough for the biggest fish swimming around the British coastline. It features the shoulder harness snap lugs, and will therefore be compatible for the stand-up method of fishing. Line capacity is approximately 415 yards of 50-lb mono.

A third option is the Ryobi S340 star drag reel. The drag settings can be a little 'soft', but the light weight of the reel makes it a pleasure to fish with all day. The largest fish I have so far landed with the S340 was a 160-lb common skate. Finally, if you must have a lever drag, the Shimano TLD25 sports the reel lugs for shoulder harness, and has the typical silky smooth drag of all the Shimano range. I have been very pleased with mine. This gives a choice of one good rod and a selection of reels that should cover every eventuality when you are halibut and big skate fishing.

Rods and Reels

For the average size of thornback skate, small-eyed ray etc when downtide fishing you need look no further than the Conoflex range of boat rods. I have a Conoflex 30-lb glass blank, so old that I wouldn't like to date it, but it has taken two marlin over 120lb, a 130-lb thresher shark, and the 160-lb common mentioned above. It's pleasant to use, and hoops round into a bend with a nice fish on. I'd rather have this type of action than something that handles like a converted broomstick!

Another good 30-lb rod blank comes from North Western. The blanks are two-piece, spigotted to provide a detachable handle. There is a fixed-reel-seat carbon winch fitting with screw-locking stainless steel caps. To upgrade a bit with the same manufacturer, go to the carbon/kevlar 30-lb IGFA boat rod. It is 8ft, and has a detachable handle. It has a chromed brass winch fitting and slotted gimbal. This blank is finished with a choice of guides. For standard fishing techniques you could use one with seven Fuji BNHG guides for smooth passage of line. A roller tip is used to reduce friction. If you have some strong tides and thus heavy leads to contend with it can be fitted with seven Aftco rollers, ideal for wire-line use. Both Conoflex and the North Western range will be ample for any downtide fishing for rays you are likely to do in British waters. The best stand-up rod is the Calspar from America.

The choice of reels is wide open. At the top of the list I put the Shimano TLD20 lever drag, not just for its friction-free drag setting, but simply because it is a pleasure to use. This model is surely the lightest, most advanced 20-lb class lever drag on the market. Don't worry about loading it with either 20- or 30-lb line. It will carry sufficient capacity for both. It is very light and allows you to stand holding an outfit all day. The alternative in the star drag range is a Penn Senator Mariner 349H. Initially it was a wire-line reel, but I don't dislike it for standard downtiding work, and of course there is a good chance that you will be using wire. It features a chrome-plated machined one-piece cast bronze spool. It has a high gear ratio to get both leads and fish up off the bottom fast. It also takes approximately 350 yards of 30-lb dacron.

Finally Ryobi market a graphite construction lightweight star drag reel. The Ryobi S320 is an almost pocket-sized 20-lb outfit reel that can also be loaded with 30-lb mono. The heaviest fish I have landed on one was a 70-lb-plus sunfish from Crookhaven in southern Ireland. It has caught me a lot of other fish as well. Any of these will make a combination that should suit any kind of downtide fishing.

Uptiding requires different techniques and different tackle. It is used primarily on the east coast, around the Essex area, where skippers thought the hum of the current over the anchor rope and in-boat noises scared the fish. They were fishing over very shallow sandbanks, and cod, bass and rays were the target species. I can understand the theory behind the technique, but I wondered whether fish might not actually be attracted into the area by sounds. The idea is to cast upcurrent from the side of the boat, allow the lead to hit bottom, then belly out the line until a grip lead pulled tight.

Anyone who has ever tried casting away from a boat using a standard rod will confirm that it can be catastrophic, not to mention dangerous. If you don't get a bird's nest or overrun you rarely get more than a few yards away from the boat, probably not enough to make any appreciable difference. To cast further, longer rods are required—not as long as beach rods, but longer than the normal boat rod. Uptiding rods have now been developed, and they are not just good for throwing baits uptide, but also for bite detection and for the pleasure they give. Possibly the best in this range come from the North Western stable. Their models are designed and built to the criteria laid down by John Rawle, one of the pioneers of the technique. The material used is a carbon/glass/kevlar composite. The 15-in tip is carbon/glass which will absorb the movement of the boat swinging at anchor yet retain the sensitivity to indicate bites. The remainder of the blank is carbon/kevlar, which provides the lightness and toughness needed to enable an angler to play a fish in the manner needed in strong tidal flows over shallow water. Two different casting weight models are available—a 4–6-oz class and a 6–8-oz class. Shakespeare also have an uptide rod, on the lines of the Ugly Stik series, which I thought were great value for money. They are not in the same class as North Western, but ideal for uptiding in shallow bays, where the tidal flow isn't so fierce.

The 1351 'O' series uptide caster has a tough carbon-composite blank and durable stainless steel and carbon locking reel seat. With hypolon rear and fore grips, it suits leads in the 4–6-oz range. New out is the 1353 Sea Wolf Uptider. Another carbon composite rated in the 4–6-oz range, the two-piece construction features hypolon rear and fore grips, plus stainless steel reel seat. In the Shakespeare range is the 1364 Hurricane Uptider, a 9½ft rod rated to cast up to 8oz, with six lined rings to minimise friction. The blank material is carbon with a kevlar wrap.

Daiwa produce some useful uptide rods. The Carbo Whisker Uptide has speedflow-lined rings with rods casting from 2 to 8oz, and from 4 to 10oz. Both feature the free-working tip essential to bite detection and are long at 10ft. Moving up in the range is the Graphite Coil Uptide, another series of two 9ft 6-in rods fitted with Titan rings throughout. The Sensor Carbon Uptide is another from the Daiwa stable, offering value for money if you are just starting on this technique. It is 9ft 6ins long, is designed for 2–8oz, and is ideal for thornback skate fishing.

The EGU Carbon Uptide has a wide range of applications. It casts leads from 2 to 10oz, and is therefore suitable for a wide range of tidal conditions. Titan guides are fitted throughout, and it is 9ft 6in long, with a comfortable Duracork handle.

Reels for uptiding obviously have to fall within the 'casting' category. It is no use mounting a 6/0 downtide metal-spooled multiplier on to a boat-casting blank. Big spools, especially metal ones, tend to overrun easily and create a bird's nest. Even plastic-spooled multipliers can over-run, so choose a tried and tested model. The best casting reel of the larger spool models would be the Shimano TLD series, in the smaller sizes from 5 upwards. The reel was first used by west-coast striped marlin anglers who needed a decent lever drag reel that would enable them to cast off the bow at a tailing striped marlin. The bait was a 1-lb caballito, or horse mackerel, and the Shimano TLD series were ideal for the job.

For general uptiding for rays, but with a slightly limited casting distance, I would suggest that the TLD 5 and TLD 10 would suit most anglers. They also handle big fish well, and their lever drag is silky smooth. The TLD 5 weighs just over 1lb, has a 4.2 to 1 gear ratio, and has a line capacity of 350 yards of 14-lb test, 280 yards of 17-lb test, 220 yards of 20-lb test, and 170 yards of 25-lb test. The TLD 10 weighs 17 ounces, has the same gear retrieve ratio and a line capacity of 450 yards of 14-lb test, 370 yards of 17-lb test, 300 yards of 20-lb test and 250 yards of 25-lb test. The ball-bearing, titanium drag has up to twice the drag surface of traditional drags, and titanium-composite washers keep the drag cool. These are the small reels with the big fish capability.

Moving on to the real casting reels, you shouldn't use anything too small. The old ABU 5000s are good for beach casting, but they aren't suitable when it comes to pumping up a big lead and a double-figure thornback ray in a strong tidal flow. Go for the larger ABU range, with the 7000 at the top. Still among the best casting reels around, they can be fitted with a larger power handle, and they carry plenty of line—right up to 25-lb test, which is more than ample for most uptiding situations. They have a star drag. You could also try the larger ABU 9000, especially if larger blond rays are your quarry.

The Shimano Speedmaster is primarily a beach reel, and perhaps a little small for bigger rays. However, for run-of-the-mill rays they are ideal, and I certainly like the line-eating gear ratio of 6.1 to 1 and the large handle. They cast well, and being small, they marry well with most uptiding rods. Ryobi market another beach reel that can double up for light uptiding, the T2. It has a level wind, which keeps your hands free, and you don't have to worry about line lay. I use this with just 12-lb or 15-lb test, as spool capacity is not so good in heavier breaking-strain lines.

For those of you yet to master the modern multiplier, there are plenty of fixed spools available for beach work that can be pressed into operation on your first uptiding trip. They are virtually fool-proof, and more important you can cast from a simple layback position, whereas a multiplier must be cast in a sweeping arc. In the confines of a boat the fixed spool is much safer, and easier for the beginner to handle. When playing a good ray in a tide you will need to pump the rod more, and regain line on the downward stroke. The fixed spool is not geared to retrieve line under pressure as a multiplier can, but for fish up to 30lb, a smooth rod-pump will still be successful. Little has been written about boat casting with a fixed spool, but with the technical improvements available with the modern fixed spool, I feel that is the boat reel to start uptiding with. Ryobi make a cheap range if you are a beginner, but the Shimano models are much better.

With a multiplier you can leave the reel in free spool with the ratchet on when you leave the rod resting on the gunwale. This stops it being dragged overboard by a taking fish. The Shimano Baitrunner reels can also offer light resistance to a taking fish—enough to stop the rod going over the side. The largest in the Baitrunner series is certainly usable in many uptiding situations.

The other way to catch your rays is from the shore. Here, a small fish should still be regarded as a good catch—in fact I rate a ray of any size as a worthwhile catch when I am shore fishing. Tremendous improvements have been made over the last ten years to enhance the beach angler's chances of success. Surely the greatest leap forward has come in the shape of improved blank designs, allowing anglers to cast further and enjoy sport they might not otherwise have had. The best by far is the Conoflex range. This name is synonymous with beach casting, and their range of rods will suit almost every angler, and certainly every angling situation. For distance casting with a big bait you need a powerful blank, yet one you can cast smoothly with. I've tried a few of the stiffer pendulum poles with dural butts, and quite honestly their action is just too fast for me to handle. I find a through-action rod more forgiving, and it allows me to 'read' when to let the lead go in order to get the best possible distance.

The 2600 is by far the best Conoflex rod I have used, and it is ideal for big baits, yet retains enough tip sensitivity for me to ascertain when a ray has flopped on to my bait. This rod is good for low-water ray marks where, as you are pushed back on to rocks by a flooding tide, the rod has backbone enough to haul a ray up hard over the snags. If you are fishing straight from an open beach, perhaps flanked by rocks but with no appreciable snags, the 2400 will give you better sport. Scaled down from the 2600, it has better tip sensitivity, and hoops over well when you have a ray on. Personally I see no reason to try anything different.

The earliest ray rod I found suitable was the old ABU 484 Zoom Beachcaster. It had a fine tip for reading bites, and I still have one I enjoy fishing with every now and then. For ray fishing from the shore, you should aim for distance with a large bait. Powering out a couple of tiny lugworms for dabs is one thing. Punching out half a fillet of mackerel or herring is quite another!

Reels for assisting in throwing these big baits should be considered carefully. You are unlikely to reach the same distances as you would when worm fishing, and for that reason I think a choice of just three reels is sufficient. If you are a newcomer to shore fishing the fixed spool is surely a must. The best is the new Shimano tapered spool Biomaster series. Pick either of the two large models and load them with 15-lb line. You'll need a shock leader of at least 40lb, more if you intend to use the back-casting or pendulum styles. The Biomaster holds loads of line, and with a perfect line lay on the spool you should have trouble-free distance casting. Throwing a big bait is a lot easier with a fixed spool than with a multiplier—well worth considering if you are into half-mackerel baits for big skate.

In the shore multiplier range there are only two I would use. The ABU 7000 still casts well, and is tried and tested on big fish of all species. I have even had blue shark on them while fishing in the Isles of Scilly. Fitted with a power handle they are just the job for most eventualities. Then there is the Shimano Speedmaster. Better suited to the run-of-the-mill rays, the high retrieve ratio allows you to speed either your bait or a hooked fish back over the top of any snag-strewn bottom. It has a large power wind handle, but remember, once you have cranked a ray to the shore under pressure, to unclip the terminal gear, cast out with just the lead, and relay the line to make a trouble-free cast next time. Wound in under pressure, nylon monofilament stretches like an elastic band. On your next cast with a big bait you are likely to suffer a bird's nest—and they always seem to come when the fish are biting!

Lines

There are many brand of line to try. Maxima, Sylcast, Stren and Ande are but some of the brand names. My favourite for rough ground or rock fishing is Sylcast, in either the blue or sorrel colour. You will need 15–18-lb line test for rock fishing, and Sylcast is durable, with a high resistance to abrasion. My favourite for open ground fishing is Ande line, now marketed in the UK. Previously I had to get all my supplies from America. Ande have been in the business of marketing fishing line for over twenty-seven years, and have had over 400 IGFA world records for various species accepted on their line. It's soft and supple, knots down well and casts well. It has a small diameter for its line class and is available in three types. Premium is possibly the best to try, and is available in clear, pink, dark green and gun-metal. The Tournament line is primarily designed for those anglers interested in world record catches. As the British records do not need line-test samples there is no need to worry about that, but it's still good to know that the standard of Tournament line is so high. Available from 2-lb to 130-lb test, it can be purchased in large bulk spools, which is handy if you are continually losing terminal gear over rough ground. Don't spool up your entire reel. Just knot on the required length to bring the spool up to optimum measure. Finally there is the new Classic line. Reputed to be very strong, it comes in line tests from 2lb to 30lb.

When you use a shock leader, as I have already said, you need a minimum of 40lb. One of the best shock leader lines is Du Pont's Stren in gold. It's supple, and with a fine diameter, it ties to the mainline to make a small knot, with easy travel through the rings. The gold colour has never affected my ray catches during the day, and is a positive advantage at night, when you can see your terminal gear coming through the waves, allowing you to swing clear of any snags.

Swivels

There are many makes of swivel on the tackle shop stands, but Berkley make about the best. They are expensive, but they are unlikely to let you down. Always keep a selection of swivels with you, even if you pre-tie all your terminal rigs at home. Brents of Hailsham in Sussex can cover most of your swivel requirements, and I would suggest placing a bulk order, sharing the cost between friends. First you need a swivel with link attachment on to which you clip either your terminal gear or your lead. Many anglers use one for the lead, with the other tied permanently to the shock leader, allowing end tackle to be changed easily.

The Bronze Linkspring swivel comes in sizes 4/0–5, the larger being better when pendulum casting. The Bronzed American snap swivel comes in sizes 3/0–14. The Nickel American snap swivel comes in sizes 4/0–5, and the Nickel Crane Interlock snap swivel comes in sizes 5/0–6. The Berkley snap swivels, which I consider the strongest, come in several models. The straight Berkley snap swivels are available in nickel or matt black finish. The Berkley snap on its own, without the swivel, also comes in nickel or matt black. The Berkley Cross-Lok snap swivels are supplied in matt black only. These snaps are unlikely ever to open up on a power cast. Finally there is the snap itself, without the swivel, also supplied in matt black only. The snap swivels range from 18-lb test right up to 150-lb test, and the Cross-Loks from 40-lb test up to 175-lb test.

You'll also need a selection of barrel swivels. The Nickel Crane swivels come in sizes 6/0–10, ordinary bronzed barrel swivels in sizes 5/0–14, and the Berkley swivels from 50-lb test right up to 350-lb test. This should cover any requirement you have.

Booms

If there's one thing you need to remember when skate and ray fishing, it's that you need to give the fish slack line when they first take the bait. To minimise any resistance to a taking fish you need a running boom, and there are plenty of different types on the market. Again Brents of Hailsham would be a good place to buy them in bulk. There are basically two types of running booms. One holds the trace away from the mainline when you drop down a bait quickly. This prevents the trace or leader twisting up around the mainline. The other is a straight running boom with a single eyelet that has a clip for the lead.

Let's start with the single eye models. First there is the brass Kilmore boom fitted with a Delrin insert in the eye to reduce friction. Then there is the stainless steel Kilmore boom with a moulded eye. On a similar line is the Zipp slider Kilmore, made of a tough nylon with a stainless spring link which allows the lead to be attached.

Among the true running booms, there is the Eddystone nylon sea boom, 7in long, but also available in a 4½-in version. Then there is the Ashpole sea boom, very good, and made from nylon with an angled vane to hold the boom straight in the current. You could also try the old-fashioned, but still extremely practical, brass Clement's boom. This comes with a plain twisted wire eyelet, with moulded eyes or with a Delrin insert and is possibly the most popular boom. There is also a stainless steel Clement's with a quick-release link, or a brass Clement's boom in 18-swg brass wire, with plain twisted eyes, the boom arm covered in black tubing. You can also make your own booms of whatever length you wish, by using the 18-swg spring wire used for the undercarriage of model aircraft.

It is worth mentioning the revolutionary new booms marketed by Knotless Fishing Tackle Ltd. As I said in the chapter on techniques, this company is run by brothers Duncan and Brian Swinbanks on the Isle of Mull, Scotland, and provides anglers with a variety of sliding booms to cope with several different sizes of fish and numerous tackle rigs. Each product is a piece of precision engineering, designed to maximise fishing results and, more important, to allow for the rapid selection or change of rig when the need arises. The most popular for big fish is the Knotless Maxi boom, an award-winning big-fish boom for lightning-fast changes of rig. With an 80-mm nylon black body, a positive 90-degree cantilever and a Mustad snaplink, it is the best for skate or halibut fishing. The Knotless Mini boom has a 40-mm nylon black body, a negative cantilever and a Mustad snaplink, and is ideal for downtide fishing for the small species like thornback skate.

For the angler interested in a running leger rig incorporating uptiding, the Tubi boom sports an extra long anti-tangle boom 200mm or 300mm long, again with a black nylon body, Kematal tube, positive cantilever and Mustad snaplink. For running leger rigs from the beach you could try the Knotless Mini boom, or even the light line Slida. In all there are some ten different booms available in the Knotless Fishing Tackle range, and they are all worthwhile.

There is an assortment of bronzed, stainless corkscrew and buckle swivels that can be adapted into booms by pushing a stiff plastic tubing into the eye of the swivel. Then simply cut the tubing to the desired length.

Tackle

These booms are prevented from sliding on to the trace by a plastic bead resting up against the swivel. There are packs of 8-mm Supertough beads in mixed colours, from 1000 upwards. One pack obviously does a lot of anglers. They also come in 5-mm sizes. Following on from this, Glowbeads come in 8-mm, 5-mm, 7-mm and 10-mm sizes, in silver, gold or luminous green.

Traces

Trace material often causes divided opinions among anglers. Some say you definitely need wire while others, myself included, prefer heavy nylon monofilament. If you are happier using wire—and this is often the case when fishing for big common skate—try Berkley Steelon leader material. It comes in 30-ft dispenser packs, in strains from 10-lb test to 210-lb test. I advise using at least 80-lb strain. The marlin steel trolling line is also good for traces, and comes in 100-yard coils and strains from 15-lb test to 80-lb test. Stick with the 60-lb and 80-lb test for big skate. You can also buy 25-ft spools of nylon-covered stranded wire, which I personally don't like, from 8-lb test up to 200-lb test.

If you use heavy-duty nylon monofilament for traces—and I do—it will cost you much less. If it starts to show signs of wear simply cut off the rough length and tie on a new one. For common skate I use 130-lb test Ande nylon, and for small-eyed rays, blonds and thornbacks, I use 50-lb. When drifting or beach casting for thornbacks that I know are likely to be small—say under double figures—then I often use 30-lb nylon. Almost any nylon will do for the 30-lb traces, but Sylcast is about the most abrasion resistant. I stick to Ande when I fish 130-lb traces for big common skate, and have more confidence if I increase it to 200-lb in snaggy waters.

The skate's jaws are designed for crushing rather than cutting, and this is why I seldom use wire. I believe that nylon feels softer to them and may be more supple, if thicker in diameter than the wire. I tend to get less dropped runs when using heavy nylon traces.

Leads

You are also going to need a wide selection of leads to suit the varying tidal conditions. While the local tackle shops will undoubtedly meet most needs, I strongly suggest that you start to make your own. For beach fishing you are going to need two types—wired grip leads and plain bombs. The wired grip leads can be the collapsible type, which you can also make yourself by pre-drilling the lead mould. They should range in weight from about 4oz up to 10oz. Anything over 6oz is too heavy for beach casting, but is ideal for uptiding from an anchored boat.

Plain bomb leads can either be moulded with a barrel swivel in the end or an eyelet of wire. To maintain a stable pattern through the air on the cast, you need to make the plain bomb with an extended wire tail, keeping the eyelet about 4in from the lead. That prevents the flight of the lead wobbling through the air, and might give you that extra few yards of distance.

The Surfbomb moulds are a good pattern for making up plain bombs, and those manufactured by DCA Moulds give the widest choice of patterns. They offer moulds for everything from beach to boat weights in ranges from 3oz up to 2lb. They also make a conical boat lead ideally suited for straight downtide fishing, as it rests comfortably upright on the sea bed. For uptiding from a boat you need either collapsible wires that fold up when you strike or fixed wires that have the wire coming out of the nose rather than the side of the lead. These are sometimes called Dungeness leads. The wires can be bent round at varying angles to suit tidal conditions, and are more practical from a boat as the retrieve is vertical and the wires are free from snagging the sand as you wind in. When retrieving from the beach the lead is dragged laterally and continually catches the bottom.

Full details on how to mould your leads safely is generally supplied with DCA moulds.

Rod Support

The shore angler needs a rod support. There are many tripods and monopods on the market, but for ray fishing I suggest using a tripod. Good ray fishing rarely comes from a wide open beach. I always seem to fish for ray from rocks or large stones, and there is no way a monopod can be used on that! The tripod is more adaptable, particularly during calm weather or from rock platforms where they can be held down low for better bite detection.

Lamps

For illumination try either the Hippolito pressure lamp or the Anchor lamp. The latter gives about 400 candlepower and is good if you are prepared to overhaul it frequently. It is also a lot cheaper than the Hippolito. Both lamps, when running properly, give a good six or eight hours of light, which is useful since much of the best ray fishing from the shore will be during the hours of darkness.

Tackle

The sun sets, and a boat angler carefully drops a bait downtide after that last ray. Shore anglers get better sport when fishing after dark.

Record Lists

While the members of the skate and ray family are not the hardest fighting fish, they are still recorded in both British and world standards. The world records are held by the International Game Fish Association (IGFA), 3000 East Las Olas Boulevard, Fort Lauderdale, Florida, USA. They used to hold records on various line-class strengths, and recently expanded them to take into account all the freshwater species, plus both saltwater and fly-fishing categories. But they record only true game fish, which in the case of skates and rays means just the halibut. The British Record (Rod-Caught) Fish Committee of the National Anglers Council lists the British record for each species, irrespective of what strength line the angler was using.

I expect the IGFA world listings eventually to expand into all the desired rod-caught species, and then we should see skates and stingrays on the lists. Should you wish to join, the IGFA do sterling work in the upkeep of world record listings, and produce a bimonthly newsletter and a yearly book full of updates on catches and other 'fishy' information. Below are the records as they stood when this book was compiled. For up-to-date record listings, contact the IGFA at the above address, or the British Record Fish Committee, 11 Cowgate, Peterborough, PE1 1LZ. The British record list is divided into boat and shore sections.

British Boat-Caught Records

Common Skate. 227lb. 1986. R. Banks. 8 miles off Tobermory, Inner Hebrides, Scotland.
Halibut. 234lb. 1979. C. Booth. Dunnet Head, off Scrabster, Scotland.
Ray, Blond. 37lb 12oz. 1973. H. Pout. Off Start Point, Devon.
Ray, Bottle-Nosed. 76lb. 1970. R. Bulpitt. The Needles, Isle of Wight.
Ray, Cuckoo. 5lb 11oz. 1975. V. Morrison. Off Causeway Coast, Northern Ireland.

Record Lists

Ray, Eagle. 61lb 8oz. M. Drew. Culver, Isle of Wight.
Ray, Electric. 96lb 1oz. 1975. N. J. Cowley, off Dodman Point, Cornwall.
Ray, Marbled Electric. 2lb 8oz. 1983. B. Maguire. Jersey, Channel Islands.
Ray, Sandy. 2lb. Qualifying weight.
Ray, Small-Eyed. 16lb 6oz. 1982. J. Lush. Minehead, Somerset.
Ray, Spotted. 8lb 3oz. 1989. G. Brownlie. Isle of Whithorn.
Ray, Sting. 61lb 8oz. 1979. V. Roberts. Cardigan Bay, Wales.
Ray, Thornback. 38lb. 1935. J. Patterson. Rustington, Sussex.
Ray, Undulate. 21lb 4oz. 1987. S. Titt. Swanage, Dorset.

British Shore-Caught Records

Common Skate. 133lb 8oz. Lochaline Pier, Sound of Mull, Scotland.
Halibut. 10lb. Qualifying weight.
Ray, Blond. 32lb 8oz. 1986. C. Reeves. Alderney, Channel Islands.
Ray, Bottle-Nosed. 15lb. Qualifying weight.
Ray, Cuckoo. 4lb 10oz. 1981. C. Wills. North Cliffs, Cornwall.
Ray, Eagle. 15lb. Qualifying weight.
Ray, Electric. 52lb 11oz. 1980. M. Wills. Porthallow, Cornwall.
Ray, Marbled Electric. 5lb 8oz. 1988. Jersey, Channel Islands.
Ray, Sandy. 2lb. Qualifying weight.
Ray, Small-Eyed. 14lb 8oz. 1989. T. Pooley. Plymouth, Devon.
Ray, Spotted. 8lb 5oz. 1980. D. Bowen. Mewslade Bay, South Wales.
Ray, Sting. 53lb 8oz. 1987. D. Harris. St Osyth's Beach, Essex.
Ray, Thornback. 21lb 12oz. 1985. S. Ramsay. Kirkudbright, Scotland.
Ray, Undulate. 21lb 4oz. 1983. K. Skinner. Jersey, Channel Islands.

IGFA World Line Class Halibut Records

Men.
2lb class. Vacant.
4lb class. Vacant.
8lb class. 8lb. 1982. P. Kogebohn. Holsteinborg, Greenland.
12lb class. 51lb. 1982. P. Kogebohn. Holsteinborg, Greenland.
16lb class. 35lb. 1985. D. Angerman. Massachusetts, USA.
20lb class. 13lb 5oz. 1986. B. Jerdmyr. Trondelag, Norway.
30lb class. 69lb. 1987. B. Monte, Jr. Massachusetts, USA.
50lb class. 228lb 4oz. 1987. E. Parett. Massachusetts, USA.
80lb class. 250lb. 1981. L. Sirard. Massachusetts, USA.
Women.
2lb class. Vacant.
4lb class. Vacant.
8lb class. Vacant.

12lb class. 12lb 2oz. 1982. K. Graul. Holsteinborg, Greenland.
16lb class. 6lb 13oz. 1982. K. Graul. Holsteinborg, Greenland.
20lb class. Vacant.
30lb class. 23lb 14oz. 1982. K. Graul. Holsteinborg, Greenland.
50lb class. 14lb 8oz. 1982. K. Graul. Holsteinborg, Greenland.
80lb class. Vacant.
130lb class. Vacant.